Northern Ireland 1921-1974:
A Select Bibliography

Garland Reference Library of Social Science (Vol. 2)

Also by Richard R. Deutsch

NORTHERN IRELAND 1968-1973:
A Chronology of Events,
Vol. I and Vol. II

Northern Ireland 1921-1974:
A Select Bibliography

Richard R. Deutsch
Maitre des Lettres,
Sorbonne University, Paris

Garland Publishing, Inc., New York & London

1975

Library of Congress Cataloging in Publication Data

Deutsch, Richard.
    Northern Ireland 1921-1974.

    Includes index.
    1. Northern Ireland--Bibliography. I. Title.
Z2043.N6D48   016.9415   75-5516
ISBN 0-8240-1060-4

C O N T E N T S

INTRODUCTION

Since 1968, communal strife in Northern Ireland and attempts
to control it have presented newspapermen with practically every major
journalistic challenge they can expect to meet in a life time. Repor-
ters have had to record and analyse the rise and fall of governments
and political leaders, the progress of a guerilla war and a colonial
administration, a campaign of sectarian assassinations which claimed
hundreds of lives and a general strike which brought down a unique community government, not to mention the suspension of civil liberties in
the form of internment without trial, military repression on a scale
never known in the British Isles and the greatest enforced population
movement since the second world war. All this against the background
of the fast changing fortunes of literally dozens of political groupings, and the apparently unchangeable prejudices and aspirations of
Northern Ireland's divided population of only one and a half million
people.

For 50 years the same people had lived in relative if uneasy
harmony under a seemingly permanent government elected by the million
people who aspired to political and cultural union with Great Britain,
and reluctantly tolerated by the half a million who aspired to an Irish
identity and culture. What went wrong ? What happened to cause the system to collapse in such chaos and provide newspapermen and political
commentators with so many million words of copy ?

Such questions can only be answered satisfactorily by the
historian. The journalist can report and analyse the immediate events,
but only the historian can draw the strands together in the perspective
of time, and analyse in depth the progress of the two communities through the centuries to the point where they reached for each other's throats.
Only the historian can properly identify the political, religious and
cultural pressures which cause and dictated the extent of the conflict.

As yet no historian has attempted a serious analysis of Northern Ireland's evolution since its creation as a state in 1921, much
less its headlong descent into barely controlled anarchy since 1968.And
before now there has not even been an attempt to catalogue the political literature of that time, and the unique proliferation of books, ma-
gazines, pamphlets and political journals of the last seven years.

Richard Deutsch has however detected the omission and has produced a catalogue which will provide an invaluable service to the student and historian seeking to master the complexity of Northern Ireland's
turbulent experiences in a way the journalist can never hope to do. He
has laid the cornerstone for future studies of a community disaster
which will provide a microcosm of practically every political phenomenon which has troubled Western Europe in this century.

Conor O'Clery

Northern Editor

The Irish Times

I

P R E F A C E

       An Irish critic reviewing the umpteenth book on the present
" troubles " in Northern Ireland wrote recently that " if all the books
already written about Northern Ireland were laid out end to end they
would bridge the gap between Catholics and Protestants ". This select
bibliography is intended as an introduction to the study of the Northern crisis which has been also affecting the Republic of Ireland since
1968 and Great Britain since 1973.Newspapers headlines round the world
have reported the day to day war in this small country of a million
and a half, they could not have explained without oversimplification
the profound divisions and aspirations of the two sides.

       A history of Northern Ireland has still to be written (See
Deutsch & Magowan p.1). This young country has not yet found its identity despite the superficial, if blatant, Protestant nationalism, torn
as it is between the traditions of its two conflicting communities, who
have more in common than meets the eye. Its history reflects this division : when one wants to dig for facts, one must resort either to Irish
or British histories as both deals with Anglo-Irish relations.

       Since 1968 numerous books and pamphlets have been published.
Few offer any analysis but most have the value of documentaries. Any
bibliography is perforce a subjective selection. The author does not
claim exhaustivity - this is not his purpose - nor does he try to emu-
late the formidable work of James Carty (See p.1.). He offers the rea-
ders sources for research in a field he has himself explored and hopes
to show the way in these uncharted waters. The emphasis is on the recent period for it is largely responsible for bringing this part of the
United Kingdom to the attention of a worldwide audience. It is also a
period the author knows well, having lived in Northern Ireland since
1966.

       From civil rights marches, the situation has developed into
a guerilla war bringing forward again the question of the very existence of that state and that of partition of the island. This is why works
of general history, dating back to the formation of the Province in
1921 , have been included.

       The bibliography covers the first and second attempts to set-
tle the Irish Question with the Anglo-Irish Treaty of 1921 and with the
Sunningdale Agreement in 1973, from the Protestant Parliament of Stormont to the first Northern Ireland Executive based on power-sharing
between Roman Catholics and Protestants. Despite the fact that pamphlets are difficult to consult abroad, (See information about micro-
film in Gracey & Howard p.2) they form a sizeable part of this bibliography. They have been included as they are an important factor in the
" troubles " themselves. The vast propaganda machine from every side
has sometimes turned the conflict into a " Paper War " (See Howard
p.2) . When necessary, background informations have been added and
cross-references indicate further reading regarding the same matter.

It is somewhat difficult to explain in a few lines the byzantine politics of this Province and any short comment on the works mentioned can hardly do them justice.

Finally the author would like to thank all those who help him very patiently, especially the staffs of the National Library of Ireland (Dublin), of the Queen's University Library (Belfast) and the Linenhall Library (Belfast). They bear no responsibility for anything published herein.

R. R. D   Belfast / Dublin

                                                             December 1974

A B B R E V I A T I O N S

For reasons of euphony the terms " Northern Ireland ", " Ulster ", " the Province " and " the North " are used interchangeably as are the terms " Republic of Ireland ", " Eire " and " the South ".

ALJ : Association for Legal Justice

BBC : British Broadcasting Corporation

CCDC : Central Citizens Defence Committee

EEC : European Economic Community

GOC NI : General Officer Commanding, Northern Ireland

ICTU : Irish Congress of Trade Unions

IRA : Irish Republican Army

ITA : Independent Television Authority

NCCL : National Council of Civil Liberties

NICRA : Northern Ireland Civil Rights Association

NUU : New University of Ulster

PR : Proportional Representation

QUB : Queen's University, Belfast

RTE : Radio Telefis Eireann

RUC : Royal Ulster Constabulary

SDLP : Social & Democratic Labour Party

UDA : Ulster Defence Association

UDI : Unilateral Declaration of Independence

UDR : Ulster Defence Regiment

USC : Ulster Special Constabulary

UVF : Ulster Volunteer Force

CHRONOLOGY

1920 : Government of Ireland Act provides for separate Parliaments and governments in Northern Ireland and Southern Ireland.

1921 : - King George V opens Northern Ireland Parliament (22 June).
- Anglo-Irish Treaty signed (6 Dec.).

1922-23 : Civil War in Southern Ireland.

1925 : Tripartite Conference on the Border.

1935 : Severe rioting in Belfast : 12 people killed (July).

1937 : New Constitution for the Irish Free State.

1939 : Irish Free State declares itself neutral in the Second World War.

1939 : IRA campaign in Great-Britain.

1949 : Irish Free State becomes the Republic of Ireland (18 Apr.).

1956 : IRA campaign against Northern Ireland.

1962 : End of the IRA campaign in Northern Ireland.

1963 : Terence O'Neill is elected Prime Minister of Northern Ireland.

1964 : Severe rioting in Belfast.

1966 : - 50th anniversary of the Dublin Easter Rising.
- UVF declares war against the IRA.

1967 : Foundation of NICRA (27 Jan.).

<u>**1968**</u> :

24 Aug. : First civil rights march in Northern Ireland.

5 Oct. : Civil rights march in Londonderry is dispersed by RUC.

9 Oct. : Foundation of People's Democracy.

<u>**1969**</u> :

1-4 Jan. : People's Democracy march between Belfast & Londonderry.

24 Feb. : General Elections in Northern Ireland.

28 Apr. : Terence O'Neill resigns.

1 May : James Chichester-Clark is elected Prime Minister of Northern Ireland.

12 Aug. : Severe rioting in Londonderry following an Orangemen march.

14 Aug. : British troops are sent in Londonderry to restore peace.

19 Aug. : Downing St Declaration setting out the British Government responsibilities for the people of Northern Ireland and the policies agreed between the two governments for the administration of the Province.

10 Sept. : Peace-Line erected in Belfast.

11 Oct. : Severe rioting in Belfast.

December : The IRA splits into two wings : Provisionals & Officials.

1970 :

11 Jan. : Sinn Fein splits into Provisional SF & Official SF.

April - May : " Arms Crisis " in the Republic of Ireland .

18 June : UK General Elections : Conservative Government headed by
Edward Heath takes over.

3-5 July : British troops impose a " curfew " in the Lower Falls of
Belfast.

21 Aug. : Foundation of the SDLP.

1971 :

Jan. : Severe rioting in Belfast.

6 Feb. : First British soldier killed in action in Belfast.

20 March : James Chichester-Clark resigns.

23 March : Brian Faulkner is elected Prime Minister of Northern Ireland.

16 July : SDLP boycotts the Northern Ireland Parliament.

9 Aug. : Introduction of internment without trial in Northern Ireland.

25 Nov. : Harold Wilson,Labour Leader, proposes a 15 point plan for peace in Ireland.

1972 :

30 Jan. : " Bloody Sunday " : 13 civilians are shot dead by British
troops in Londonderry.

24 March : Direct Rule : Edward Heath, Prime Minister of Great-Britain,
prorogues the Northern Ireland Parliament. The Province is
administered directly from Westminster.

25 March : William Whitelaw is appointed Secretary of State for Northern
Ireland.

June - July : Loyalists barricade areas of Belfast and some towns in the
Province .

26 June - 9 July : Provisional IRA Truce.

21 July : " Bloody Friday " : 21 bombs planted by the Provisional IRA
explode in Belfast killing 9 persons.

31 July : " Operation Motorman " : British Army enters all republican
" No - Go areas ".

25-27 Sept. : Darlington Conference in England.

30 Oct. : Publication of the British " Green Paper " : it recognizes the
" Irish Dimension " of the Northern problem.

19 Nov. : Sean MacStiofain, Provisional IRA Chief of Staff, is arrested
by Irish police in Dublin.

1 Dec. : - Two car-bombs explode in Dublin killing two persons.
- The Irish Parliament vote strong anti-IRA law.

<u>1973</u> :

7 Feb. : Loyalist strike in Northern Ireland.

28 Feb. : General Elections in the Republic of Ireland : William Cosgrave is elected Prime Minister and leads a coalition government (Labour - Fine Gael).

8 March : - Referendum on the Border in Northern Ireland.
- IRA car-bombs kill one person in London.

20 March : Publication of the British " White Paper ".

28 June : Elections in Ulster for the Northern Ireland Assembly.

10 Sept. : Trial opens in Winchester (England) of people suspected
to have planted car-bombs in London on March 8,1973.

16 Sept. : Tommy Herron, one of the UDA leaders, is found shot dead.

17 Sept. : Meeting in Dublin of Edward Heath, Prime Minister of Great-
Britain, and Wlliam Cosgrave, Prime Minister of the Irish
Republic.

31 Oct. : Three IRA leaders escape in helicopter from Mountjoy Prison,
Dublin.

22 Nov. : Northern Ireland Executive is announced.

6-9 Dec. : Sunningdale Conference in England.

<u>1974</u> :

1 Jan. : Northern Ireland Executive officially takes up duty.

7 Jan. : Brian Faulkner, NI Chief Executive, resigns from the Unionist
Party.

23 Jan. : Official Unionist Party, Ulster Vanguard and Democratic Unionist Party formally withdraw from the NI Assembly.

4 Feb. : IRA bomb placed in a British Army coach kills 12 people in
Yorkshire.

28 Feb.: UK General Elections : Harold Wilson elected Prime Minister
heads a Labour Government.

5 March : Merlyn Rees is appointed Secretary of State for Northern Ireland.

4 Apr. : British Labour Government announces its programme for Ulster.

5 May : Brian Faulkner founds the Unionist Party of Northern Ireland.

14 May : Ulster Workers Council declares a general strike in Ulster.

17 May : 30 people are killed in the Irish Republic by car-bombs in
Dublin & Monaghan.

28 May : Brian Faulkner, NI Chief Executive, resigns. The NI Assembly
collapses.

29 May : UWC ends strike.

3 June : IRA prisoner dies after a 65 days' hunger strike in British Jail.

17 June : Bomb explodes at the British Houses of Parliament in London.

4 July : British Governments publishes a " White Paper " to propose a Constitutional Convention in Ulster.

17 July : Bomb explodes at the Tower of London , one person is killed.

2 Sept. : Expansion of the RUC, RUC Reserve and the UDR.

11 Sept.: William Cosgrave, Prime Minister of the Irish Republic,meets Harold Wilson, Prime Minister of Great-Britain, in London.

10 Oct. : UK General Elections : Labour Government wins.

15 Oct. : Severe rioting in Long Kesh Internment camp.

21 Nov. : Bombs in Birmingham kill 21 persons.

29 Nov. : British Parliament introduces the Prevention of Terrorism (Temporary Provisions) Act.

10 Dec. : Protestant clergymen meet secretly Provisional IRA leaders at Feakle, Co Clare, in the Irish Republic.

20 Dec. : The Provisional IRA announces an 11 day Christmas Truce to start on December 22, 1974.

<u>SECTION A : NON - FICTION</u>

1 - BIBLIOGRAPHIES & REFERENCE WORKS

CARTY, James : Bibliography of Irish History. 1912 - 1921 .
1936. Dublin. Stationery Office. p.177

Standard work.Valuable notes appended to various entries.

CHUBB, Basil (ed.) : A source book of Irish government.
1964. Dublin. Institute of Public Administration.

Standard work.

DARBY, John P : Register of research into the Irish conflict.
1972. Belfast. Northern Ireland Community Relations Commission. p.34

Detailed compilation of about 200 theses.

DEUTSCH, Richard & MAGOWAN, Vivien : Northern Ireland 1968 - 1973 .
A Chronology of events.
Vol. I : 1968 - 1971 .1973. Belfast.Blackstaff Press. p.180
Vol.II : 1972 - 1973 .1974. Belfast.Blackstaff Press. p.228

A daily account of the period 1968 - 1973. The chronology
is based on contemporary speeches, official statements, statistics, newspaper reports, interviews, TV & radio broadcasts.
The two volumes record the main events of each day. See also
in Appendices : Tables of Northern Ireland Cabinet Ministers
of the Stormont Government (from 25.3.1963 to 24.3.1972)
and the list of members elected to the Northern Ireland Assembly on June 30, 1973. Both volumes are fully indexed.

DUDLEY EDWARDS, Ruth : An atlas of Irish History.
1973. London. Methuen / New-York. Harper & Row. p.261

74 maps & graphs outlining the history of Ireland from the
earliest times to the present day in visual form, with short
complementary text.

EAGER, A.R : A guide to Irish bibliographical material. Being a bibliography of Irish bibliographies and sources of information.
1964. London. Library Association.

ELLIOTT, Sydney : Northern Ireland Parliamentary elections results.
1921 - 1972 .
1973. Chichester. Political Reference Publications.

Valuable work of reference.

FREEMAN, T.W : Ireland.A general & regional geography.
1950. London. Methuen. 1972 (revised ed.) p.560

Standard work by a leading geographer - See also FREEMAN in
Relevant chapters Section .

GRACEY, James & HOWARD, Paula : <u>Northern Ireland political literature</u>
<u>1968 - 1970</u> . pp.44 - 82. Part 1 .
1971. Belfast. <u>Irish Booklore</u>. Vol.1 No 1

A bibliography of ephemeral literature of the present troubles. Part 2 in Volume 2 is due in 1975.
The Belfast Linenhall Library houses the best collection of
pamphlets, broadsheets, posters, etc... produced by the various political parties, groups and associations in Ireland
during the present crisis.
The Irish University Press has microfilmed part of this collection . Details are available from IUP, 81 Merrion Square,
Dublin.1 .

HAYES, R. J (ed.) : <u>Manuscript sources for the history of Irish Civili-</u>
<u>sation</u> .
1966. Boston (Mass.). 11 vols.

Extremely valuable for detailed research.

HOWARD Paula : <u>The Paper War</u>.
1974. Belfast. <u>Fortnight Magazine</u> No 75 - 79 .

A series of articles on political propaganda sheets and the
fringe press in Northern Ireland since 1969. An excellent
introduction to the local publications which concern the
political situation. The series covers official organs; republican & loyalist publications; communism & socialism and
the People's Democracy and the Civil Rights Association.

JOHNSTON, Edith M : <u>Irish History - A select bibliography</u> .
1972. (revised ed.) London. The Historical Association.
p.76

KNIGHT, James & BAXTER-MOORE, Nicolas : <u>Northern Ireland Local Govern-</u>
<u>ment elections : 30 May 1973</u> .
1973. London. Arthur McDougall Fund. p.107

Results for each district electoral area arranged in party
order.

MAGEE, John : <u>Northern Ireland : crisis & conflict</u> .
1974. London / Boston . Routledge & Kegan Paul. p.196

A reader . Good but short introduction to the present crisis .

MEALLY Victor (ed.) : <u>Encyclopedia of Ireland</u> .
1968. Dublin. Allen Figgis. p. 463

Intended for the general reader, this work provides some
useful information for the student of Irish history.

MALTBY, Arthur : <u>The Government of Northern Ireland 1922 - 1972</u> .
<u>A catalogue & breviate of parliamentary papers.</u>
1974. Dublin. Irish University Press. p. 235

Source book with no commentary. A series of summaries of Northern Ireland Command Papers and departmental reports between
1921 & 1972. Essential reading despite a few omissions.

MOODY, T. W (ed.) : Irish Historiography - 1936 - 1970 .
1971. Dublin. Irish committee of Historical Sciences. 155 p.

See especially Chap VII : Twentieth-century Ireland. 1914 -
1970.

NORTH EASTERN BOUNDARY BUREAU : Handbook of the Ulster Question.
1923. Dublin. Stationery Office. 164 p. & maps.

The director of the North Eastern Boundary Bureau described this work as " a compendium of facts, many of which are
not generally realized, for all those interested in the Ulster Question ". The introduction clearly states that " the
conclusions drawn from these facts and figures, viewed from
every angle, are against any form of Partition, and particularly against the form of Partition set up by the Act of
1920. "
Essential reading.

QUECKETT, Sir Arthur : The Constitution of Northern Ireland.
1928. Belfast. HMSO. Part 1
1933. Belfast. HMSO. Part 2
1946. Belfast. HMSO. Part 3

REPORT OF THE IRISH BOUNDARY COMMISSION. 1925.
1969. Shannon. Irish University Press. 169 p. & maps.

Findings of the abortive boundary commission set up by the
Anglo-Irish Treaty of 1921. The Report was suppressed by
agreement between British, Irish and Northern Ireland governments and was made public only in 1968.
Before the Award of the Commission was announced, " leaks "
of its contents provoked a major political crisis in the
Irish Free State. The Report is extremely valuable for its
informations about social and economic conditions in the Border areas in the early years of the Partition. See especially the sections relating to the decision of not handing the
areas of Londonderry and Newry to the Irish Free State.
Essential reading.

SIMMS, Samuel : The Orange Society : a select bibliography. pp.2-9
in Irish Book Lover. 1937. Dublin. Vol.25

SMITH, Howard : Ireland - Some episodes from her past.
1974. London. BBC Publications. 136 p.

Following the success of a series of 10 television program-
mes broadcast by the BBC in 1971, the producer published
this collection of essays which concentrate on those events,
movements and personalities in the past which still have some
influence today. A good introduction for those who have no
previous knowledge of Irish history.

<u>ULSTER YEAR BOOK</u> :
   Belfast. HMSO. Published since 1926.

   Official publication : useful for reference (statistics,
   informations on central and local governments,etc..)
   Bibliographies.

<u>WHO'S WHO, WHAT'S WHAT & WHERE IN IRELAND</u> :
   1973. London / Dublin. G.Chapman / Irish Times. p.736

   This work covers The Republic of Ireland and Northern
   Ireland . There are over 3,500 entries and short texts
   about the government, the judiciary , the education,
   the tax systems, the health services, the social welfare, etc.. of the two countries.

2 - OFFICIAL PUBLICATIONS

A - UNITED KINGDOM :

All material has been published by Her Majesty's Stationery Office in Belfast, unless otherwise stated.

FLAGS & EMBLEMS (DISPLAY) ACT (N.I) 1954 :
1954. p.4

The Union Jack is the lawful flag to be flown in Northern Ireland. Any other emblems (i.e. the Tricolour Flag of the Irish Republic) has to be removed and the police has a right to do so. Since the beginning of the present crisis a number of flags have been flown without any person charged. For example, one sees now in some loyalist areas more Ulster Flags and Vanguard Flags than Union Jacks.

BELFAST REGIONAL SURVEY AND PLAN 1963 :
1963. p.257

Terence O'Neill, then Northern Ireland Prime Minister, wanted to " transform the face of Ulster " by implementing the proposals of Professor R. Matthew . The plan suggested the link-up of two provincial towns ; Portadown & Lurgan, to form a new city, to be called Craigavon. The new town was to have 100,000 inhabitants by 1981 .

BELFAST REGIONAL SURVEY & PLAN : Recommendations and conclusions.
1965. (Cmd 451)

ECONOMIC DEVELOPMENT IN NORTHERN IRELAND :
1965 (reprinted 1967) (Cmd 479) p.153

Most of the document is Professor T. Wilson's (economic consultant) detailed report.

THE RE-SHAPING OF LOCAL GOVERNMENT : STATEMENT OF AIMS .
1967 (reprinted 1968) (Cmd 517) p.33

See in appendices : statistics and a short bibliography of background sources and recent academic works relevant to the subject.

THE CONSTITUTION OF NORTHERN IRELAND : Being the Government of Ireland Act, 1920, as amended to 31 December 1968 .
1968. p.61

UNITED KINGDOM COMMISSION ON THE CONSTITUTION. Written evidence No 3 .
The Home Office (Note on the status of Northern Ireland within the United Kingdom) and the Government Departments of Northern Ireland.
1969. London. HMSO.

See also the conclusions of the Commission in the Kilbrandon Report published in London in November 1973.

RE-SHAPING OF LOCAL GOVERNMENT : FURTHER PROPOSALS.
Sept. 1969 (Cmd 530) p.36

Proposals include the abolition of plural voting, to provide for universal adult franchise in local government elections. See also appendices for list of existing local authorities and the populations, areas and rateable values of the proposed new areas.

DISTURBANCES IN NORTHERN IRELAND : REPORT OF THE CAMERON COMMISSION.
Sept. 1969 (Cmd 532) p.124 and maps.

Also known as the Cameron Report.
Official inquiry into the origins of the civil rights campaign. Covers from August 1968 to April 1969 .Detailed survey of the organisations involved in the disturbances : Northern Ireland Civil Rights Association; People's Democracy; Derry Citizens Action Committee ; the IRA and minor Republican organisations; the Ulster Constitution Defence Committee and the Ulster Protestant Volunteers (both organized by the Reverend Ian Paisley in 1966).
The Report found a " failure of leadership on all sides " which allowed tensions to build up and eventually to explode in violence. It also suggested setting up an independent tribunal to investigate complaints related to the police, and a change in the method of appointment of senior local government officials.

A COMMENTARY BY THE GOVERNMENT OF NORTHERN IRELAND TO ACCOMPANY THE CAME-RON REPORT.
Sept. 1969 (Cmd 534) p.17

It incorporates an account of measures already taken by the Government of Northern Ireland to meet legitimate demands and it outlines a programme of action. It refers to the setting up on August 26, 1969 of an advisory board under Baron Hunt to examine the Royal Ulster Constabulary and the Ulster Special Constabulary (See Hunt Report), and to the setting up on August 27, 1969, of a tribunal under Mr Justice Scarman to inquire into the civil disturbances between April and August 1969 (See Scarman Report).

REPORT OF THE ADVISORY COMMITTEE ON POLICE IN NORTHERN IRELAND :
Oct.1969 (Cmd 535) p.50

Also known as the Hunt Report.
It recommends a reform of the Royal Ulster Constabulary : it should be relieved of all duties of a military nature and backed by a volunteer reserve force. The auxiliary force of the Ulster Special Constabulary (also known as the B-Specials) was to be replaced by a 4,000 strong locally recruited force under the control of the General Officer in Commandant of the British Army in Northern Ireland.
The Hunt Report was published on Friday 10 October and severe rioting spread in Belfast during the week-end in protest to its recommendations.Two civilians and one policeman were kil-

led in the Protestant district of the Shankill Road area of Belfast. British troops had opened fire on civilian snipers operating against them in this district.

ROYAL ULSTER CONSTABULARY RESERVE :
    1969 (Cmd 536) 4 p.

Details about the setting up of this new force (See the Hunt Report) include that members would not be issued with arms and would have to take an Oath of Allegiance. Initial establishment would be 1,500. In September 1974, the Secretary of State for Northern Ireland,Merlyn Rees, made provisions to increase the force up to 6,000, including 1,500 women.

TEXT OF A COMMUNIQUE ISSUED FOLLOWING DISCUSSIONS BETWEEN THE SECRETARY OF STATE FOR THE HOME DEPARTMENT AND THE NORTHERN IRELAND GOVERNMENT IN BELFAST ON 9 & 10 OCTOBER 1969.
    1969. London. HMSO. (Cmnd 4178) 8 p.

The agreement between Stormont Cabinet Ministers and James Callaghan regarding the measures of reforms. It contains the decisions that the RUC should be unarmed, that a minister for Community Relations should be appointed and that a Bill would be introduced to establish a Commissioner for Complaints.

FORMATION OF THE ULSTER DEFENCE REGIMENT :
    Nov. 1969. London. HMSO. (Cmnd 4188)

Proposals for the setting up of the new 6,000 strong Defence Force to replace the Ulster Special Constabulary (See also the Hunt Report). Recruitment started in January 1970 and the Regiment took up its duties on April 30, 1970.

REGULATIONS FOR THE ULSTER DEFENCE REGIMENT. Army Code No 60589
    1969. London.

See also the Hunt Report.

THE WAY AHEAD. STORMONT :
    1969.

Leaflet on new measures and reforms.

NOTES ON NORTHERN IRELAND.
    1969.

Leaflet.

REPORT OF THE COMMITTEE ON THE SUPREME COURT OF JUDICATURE OF NORTHERN IRELAND.
    March 1970. (Cmd 4292).

NORTHERN IRELAND COMMISSIONER FOR COMPLAINTS : FIRST REPORT.
    1970. (H.C.2001)

The first Commissioner, John Benn, took up his duties on December 22, 1969.

NORTHERN IRELAND DEVELOPMENT PROGRAMME : 1970 - 1975 .
1970. 227 p. & maps.

Report of three consultants : Prof. Jack Parkinson; Prof.
Robert Matthew and Prof. Thomas Wilson.

REPORT OF THE REVIEW BODY ON LOCAL GOVERNMENT IN NORTHERN IRELAND.
1970. (Cmd 546) 68 p.

Also known as the Macrory Report.

A RECORD OF CONSTRUCTIVE CHANGE.
Aug. 1971. (Cmd 558) 14 p.

The Stormont Government's reforms introduced since 1969 to
implement equality of treatment and freedom from discrimination.

THE FUTURE DEVELOPMENT OF THE PARLIAMENT AND GOVERNMENT OF NORTHERN
IRELAND.
Oct.1971. (Cmd 560) 12 p.

A consultative document (a " green paper ") ruling out the
use of Proportional Representation but suggesting 20 to 30
additional MPs at the Stormont Parliament. It also criticizes the policy of boycott of the Northern Ireland Parliament
by the SDLP started on July 16, 1971.

REPORT OF THE ENQUIRY INTO THE ALLEGATIONS AGAINST THE SECURITY FORCES
OF PHYSICAL BRUTALITY IN NORTHERN IRELAND, ARISING OUT OF
THE EVENTS OF 9th AUGUST, 1971.
Nov. 1971. London. HMSO. (Cmd 4823). 73 p.

Also known as the Compton Report.
On August 9, 1971 the British Government introduced adminis-
trative internment in Northern Ireland and 342 men were arrested. By noon on November 10, 980 men had been detained. A certain number of persons released complained of " tortures "
from the British Army. The report denies that brutality was
used during the interrogation of detainees but records " ill-
treatment " and instances methods used such as holding, the
use of continuous noise, posturing against the wall for up to
six hours and a diet of bread and water as well as deprivation
of sleep. In 1974 the British Government paid substantial compensations to several persons who had been detained and inter-
rogated during the first week of internment.
See also : MacGUFFIN in Selected Works section.

REPORT OF THE COMMITTEE OF PRIVY COUNSELLORS APPOINTED TO CONSIDER AUTHO-
RISED PROCEDURES FOR THE INTERROGATION OF PERSONS SUSPECTED
OF TERRORISM.
March 1972. London. HMSO. (Cmnd 4901). 24 p.

Also known as the Parker Report.
The committee was not unanimous in its finding on the methods
used in interrogating detainees in Northern Ireland. Lord
Parker in a majority report thought they were justified in

exceptional circumstances. In a minority report, Lord Gardiner thought they were illegal. At Westminster, the Prime Minister, Edward Heath, accepted the report and said that the techniques examined by the Committee (See the Compton Report) would not be used in future in interrogation.
See also MacGUFFIN in Selected Works section.

REPORT OF THE TRIBUNAL APPOINTED TO INQUIRE INTO THE EVENTS ON SUNDAY 30 JANUARY 1972, WHICH LED TO LOSS OF LIFE IN CONNECTION WITH THE PROCESSION IN LONDONDERRY ON THAT DAY :
April 1972. London. HMSO. (H.L.101 / H.C.220) p.45 and map.

Also known as the Widgery Report.
The march held by the NICRA on that day in Londonderry was prohibited under an order made on August 9th, 1971.
Lord Widgery found generally that the British Army had only fired after being subjected to gunfire. NICRA was blamed for organizing the march. Lord Widgery was unconvinced that the 13 civilians who died had been armed or carried nail-bombs. In December 1974, the British Government announced that it would pay compensations to relatives of the victims and to the 13 injured persons.

VIOLENCE & CIVIL DISTURBANCES IN NORTHERN IRELAND IN 1969 :
April 1972. (Cmd 566)
Vol.1 : Report. p.247
Vol.2 : Appendices & maps. p.60

Also known as the Scarman Report.
The report analyzes the civil disturbances between March and August 1969. It finds that there had been no plot to overthrow the Stormont Government nor any evidence of an armed insurrection. Violent actions had been planned by both Protestants and Republicans. The report criticizes the Royal Ulster Constabulary but said that they were not a partisan force.

NORTHERN IRELAND : FINANCIAL ARRANGEMENTS & LEGISLATION.
May 1972. London. HMSO. (Cmnd 4998)

PROPORTIONAL REPRESENTATION : NORTHERN IRELAND DISTRICT COUNCIL ELECTIONS 1972.
1972. p.5

Prefaced by the Secretary of State for Northern Ireland, William Whitelaw, this pamphlet was given out free to every household to explain the Proportional vote. It states that it would be used only for these District Council Elections. Proportional Representation was used in Northern Ireland from 1921 to 1925 and then was abolished.

THE FUTURE OF NORTHERN IRELAND : A PAPER FOR DISCUSSION .
Oct.1972. London. HMSO. p.98

Also known as " The Green Paper ".
Presented by the Secretary of State for Northern Ireland, William Whitelaw, this paper for discussion contains a turning

point in British policy towards Ireland : See especially para-
graphs 76 & 77 on the " Irish Dimension ". It made the point
that any plan in the future must take account of Northern Ireland 's close ties with the Irish Republic.
In the foreword, the Secretary of State for Northern Ireland,
William Whitelaw, explains that the object is " to find a system of government which will enjoy the support and the respect
of the overwhelming majority ".
The Appendices contain the detailed statements of the Unionist
Party, the Alliance Party , the NILP , the SDLP , the Liberal
Party and the New Ulster Movement for a new provincial assem-
bly.

REPORT OF THE COMMISSION TO CONSIDER LEGAL PROCEDURES TO DEAL WITH TERRO-
RIST ACTIVITIES IN NORTHERN IRELAND :
Dec.1972. London. (Cmd 5185) p.42

Also known as the Diplock Report.
Amongst its proposals were the changing of the onus of proof
to the accused in the case of persons charged with possessing
arms or explosives having to prove their innocence, and the
giving of power to soldiers to arrest and detain suspects for
a period of up to 4 hours while checking identification. Lord
Diplock emphasised that his recommendations should only be
implemented for as long as the emergency lasts.

NORTHERN IRELAND CONSTITUTIONAL PROPOSALS :
March 1973. London. HMSO. (Cmd 5259) p.34

Westminster's proposals for a Northern Ireland Assembly of
80 members elected by proportional representation to replace the former Stormont Parliament. It makes provision for
the setting up of a Council of Ireland for North / South
discussions on relevant matters. The Assembly would have
committees whose Chairmen would form the Executive.

REPORT & RECOMMENDATIONS OF THE WORKING PARTY ON DISCRIMINATION IN THE
PRIVATE SECTOR OF EMPLOYMENT.
May 1973. p.46

The Catholic minority in Northern Ireland always complained
bitterly of " religious discrimination " in employment, housing, etc... The report suggests a fairly complex sets of
measures to fight discrimination co-ordinated by a Fair Employment Agency.

NORTHERN IRELAND CONSTITUTION ACT. 1973. CHAPTER 36 :
July 1973. London. HMSO . p.51

The Act making new provision for the Government of Northern
Ireland, establishing the power of the new Northern Ireland
Assembly and of the Secretary of State for Northern Ireland.
It abolishes the old Stormont Parliament and the office of
Governor of Northern Ireland.

<u>NORTHERN IRELAND (EMERGENCY PROVISIONS) ACT 1973</u>. CHAPTER 53 :
July 1973. London.

It makes provision for trial by a single judge without a jury
for " terrorist-type " offences because of the possible intimidation of juries in Northern Ireland .
The Civil Authorities (Special Powers Act) of 1922 was also
repealed.

<u>NORTHERN IRELAND : AGREED COMMUNIQUE ISSUED FOLLOWING THE CONFERENCE
BETWEEN THE IRISH & BRITISH GOVERNMENTS AND THE PARTIES
INVOLVED IN THE NORTHERN IRELAND EXECUTIVE (DESIGNATE)
ON 6th, 7th, 8th, and 9th DECEMBER, 1973.</u>
Dec.1973. p.8

Also known as the Sunningdale Agreement.
The Agreement reached in the tripartite talks held in England
at Sunningdale in Berkshire. Taking part were the Prime Minister of the United Kingdom, Edward Heath ; the Prime Minister
of the Republic of Ireland, Liam Cosgrave ; and members of
the Northern Ireland Executive designate led by the Chief Executive designate, Brian Faulkner .
The Government of the Republic stated that if fully accepted
that " there could be no change in the status of Northern Ireland until a majority " desired it.
The British Government " solemnly declared " that it support-
ed the wishes of the majority in Northern Ireland and affirm-
ed that its present status was part of the United Kingdom.
" If in the future, the majority (in Northern Ireland) wis-
hed to become part of a united Ireland," the British Government would support that wish, the statement added.
Other matters agreed on included the structure and scope of
the Council of Ireland, measures for the immediate bringing
to justice by the Irish Government, of those accused of cri-
mes of violence, " however motivated ", committed in Northern Ireland. (See also <u>REPORT OF THE LAW ENFORCEMENT COM-
MISSION</u>. May 1974. in this section).
The appointment of a Police Authority by the Irish Government
would take place and there would be co-operation by both
North and South through the Council of Ireland in police matters.
The fall of the Northern Ireland Assembly on May 29, 1974
following the strike of the Ulster Workers Council is part-
ly the result of the Sunningdale Agreement. After December
1973 the Loyalists made every possible attempt to wreck the
new power-sharing Executive and to prevent the ratification
of the Agreement. (See also <u>THE NORTHERN IRELAND CONSTITU-
TION</u>. July 1974. in this section).

<u>PROSECUTIONS IN NORTHERN IRELAND . A STUDY OF FACTS</u>.
Feb.1974. London. HMSO. p.42

This report is an answer to " <u>JUSTICE IN NORTHERN IRELAND.
A STUDY IN SOCIAL CONFIDENCE</u> " (See HADDEN & HILLYARD in
Pamphlets section) which claimed that the prosecuting au-

thority were not impartial. <u>Prosecutions in Northern Ireland</u>
demonstrates that all these allegations were wrong.

REPORT OF THE LAW ENFORCEMENT COMMISSION .
  May 1974. London. HMSO. (Cmnd 5627) p.43

  In December 1973 members of the Law Enforcement Commission
were appointed by the Irish & British Governments following
the Sunningdale Conference Agreement (See paragraph 10 of
the Joint Communique).
The report found that an All-Ireland court was not a practi-
cable immediate solution. It favoured extraterritorial jurisdiction but recognized its difficulties in the present
violence.

THE NORTHERN IRELAND CONSTITUTION.
  July 1974. London. (Cmnd 5675). p.19

  Following the fall of the Northern Ireland Assembly on May
29, 1974 after the Ulster Workers Council's strike, the Secretary of State for Northern Ireland, Merlyn Rees, published this document announcing that a Convention would be
elected to decide of the future of the Province. In December 1974 it was expected that the elections would take
place in Spring 1975. In the meantime Northern Ireland was
to be administered under " direct rule " from Westminster.

NORTHERN IRELAND : FINANCE & THE ECONOMY :
  Sept.1974. London. HMSO. p.32

  The first of a series of 3 discussion papers to be published before the elections of the Northern Ireland Convention.
This document details the heavy dependence of Northern Ireland on the British Exchequer. It is very much a strong warning to those in the Province who would favour an independent Ulster.

NORTHERN IRELAND : CONSTITUTIONAL CONVENTION : PROCEDURE.
  Nov.1974. London. HMSO. p.24

  The second discussion paper. It deals mainly with the setting up and the procedure of the Northern Ireland Convention. In the Appendices there are models of Conventions
held in Ireland in 1917-18, in Newfoundland in 1946-47 and
the present Australian Constitutional Convention.

B - REPUBLIC OF IRELAND :

All material has been published in Dublin.

THE CONSTITUTION OF THE IRISH FREE STATE (SAORSTAT EIREANN) ACT
1922, AND THE PUBLIC GENERAL ACTS PASSED BY THE OIREACH-
TAS OF SAORSTAT EIREANN DURING THE YEAR OF 1922 .
1922. Stationery Office.

IRISH FREE STATE (SAORSTAT EIREANN) OFFICIAL HANDBOOK :
1932. Talbot Press. p.150 and map.

CONSTITUTION OF IRELAND 1937 :
1937 . Revised 1942. Government Publications Office. p.214

Since it became in existence in Ireland, Protestants in Northern Ireland have repeatedly asked for suppression of articles 2 , 3 and 44.
Article 2 reads : " The national territory consists of the
whole island of Ireland, its islands and the territorial
waters."
Article 3 : " Pending the re-integration of the national territory, and without prejudice to the right of the Parliament
and Government established by this Constitution to exercise
jurisdiction over the whole of that territory, the laws enac-
ted by that Parliament shall have the like area and extent
of application as the laws of Saorstat Eireann and the like
extra-territorial effect."
Article 44, paragraph II reads : " The State recognises the
special position of the Holy Catholic Apostolic and Roman
Church as the guardian of the Faith professed by the great
majority of the citizens."
On December 8, 1972 , voters in the Irish Republic decided
in a referendum by 721,003 to 133,430 in favour of the dele-
tion of the subsections of Article 44 giving a special position to the Roman Catholic Church.

REPORT OF THE COMMITTEE OF THE CONSTITUTION .
1967. Stationery Office. p.144.

LYNCH, John : SPEECHES & STATEMENTS: IRISH UNITY, NORTHERN IRELAND,
ANGLO-IRISH RELATIONS. AUGUST 1969 - OCTOBER 1971.
1971. Government Information Bureau.

The Leader of the Fianna Fail party was Prime Minister of the
Irish Republic when the present crisis started in Ulster.He
held the position from 1966 to 1973 and during that period made several important speeches on Northern Ireland.
Essential reading.

NORTHERN IRELAND : AGREED COMMUNIQUE ISSUED FOLLOWING THE CONFERENCE
BETWEEN THE IRISH & BRITISH GOVERNMENTS AND THE PARTIES
INVOLVED IN THE NORTHERN IRELAND EXECUTIVE (DESIGNATE)
ON 6th, 7th, 8th and 9th DECEMBER 1973.
Dec.1973. Government Information Services. p.8

See the Sunningdale Agreement p.11

13

3 - <u>NEWSPAPERS</u> :

Newspapers will offer much valuable information, especially for the period 1966 - 1974 .

B E L F A S T :

<u>BELFAST TELEGRAPH</u> (daily) liberal unionist

<u>BELFAST NEWSLETTER</u> (daily) unionist

<u>IRISH NEWS</u> (daily) nationalist

<u>PROTESTANT TELEGRAPH</u> . 1966 - (fortnightly) published by the Reverend Ian Paisley.

<u>FORTNIGHT MAGAZINE</u> . 1970 - (fortnightly) independent

<u>LOYALIST NEWS</u> . 1969 - (weekly) grass root's unionism

<u>FREE CITIZEN</u> . 1969 - 1971 (weekly) published by the People's Democracy. After the introduction of internment the newspaper changed its name to <u>UNFREE CITIZEN</u> (1971 -)

<u>REPUBLICAN NEWS</u>. 1970 - (weekly) grass root's republicanism.

L O N D O N :

<u>THE TIMES</u> (daily)

<u>THE DAILY TELEGRAPH</u> (daily)

<u>THE GUARDIAN</u> (daily)

<u>THE SUNDAY TIMES</u> (weekly)

<u>THE OBSERVER</u> (weekly)

<u>THE SUNDAY TELEGRAPH</u> (weekly)

D U B L I N :

<u>IRISH TIMES</u> (daily)

<u>IRISH PRESS</u> (daily)

<u>IRISH INDEPENDENT</u> (daily)

<u>THIS WEEK</u> (weekly) 1969 - 1973

<u>HIBERNIA</u> (fortnightly)

THE UNITED IRISHMAN. 1948 - (weekly) published by Sinn Fein
Gardiner St

AN PHOBLACHT . 1970 - (weekly) published by Sinn Fein Kevin
St .

THE IRISH PEOPLE . 1973 - (weekly) published by the Irish
Civil Rights Association.

4 - GENERAL WORKS

BECKETT, J. C : <u>The making of modern Ireland. 1603 - 1923.</u>
1966. London. Faber & Faber. p.496

Good introduction to the subject . Bibliography.

BUCKLAND, Patrick : <u>The Anglo-Irish & the new Ireland. 1855 - 1922</u> .
1972. Dublin / New-York . Gill & Macmillan. p. 363

The role played by Southern unionism in the Irish Question.

BUCKLAND, Patrick : <u>Ulster Unionism and the origins of Northern Ireland</u> .
<u>1886 - 1922</u> .
1973. Dublin / New-York. Gill & Macmillan. p.207

The author deals with three themes :
The emergence of Ulster Unionism as a strong political force;
the establishment in Ireland of a separate state within the
UK; the tragic division in the Northern Ireland community .

BUCKLAND, Patrick : <u>Irish Unionism. 1885 - 1923 . A documentary history.</u>
1973. Belfast. HMSO. p. 397

Documents from the Public Record Office of Northern Ireland
explaining Irish Unionists objections to Home Rule.
Valuable background reading.

CULLEN, L. M : <u>An economic history of Ireland since 1660</u> .
1972. London. Batsford. p.208

There are few economic studies on Ireland and this one is a
basic work. Last chapter takes the story up to 1971.Biblio-
graphy and important notes on primary sources.

DAVIS, Richard : <u>Arthur Griffith & non-violent Sinn Fein</u> .
1974. Anvil Books. Tralee. p. 232

Valuable history of the evolution of Sinn Fein . Good analysis of Arthur Griffith's ideas of revolution through pas-
sive resistance and a dual monarchy settlement which would
bridge the gap between the different Irish traditions.

EVANS, E. E : <u>The personality of Ireland.</u>
1973. London. Cambridge. University Press. p. 123

A leading geographer 's analysis of Ireland, based original-
ly on the text of four lectures delivered in Belfast in 1972.
The author deals with habitat, heritage and history.
Useful work to understand the Irish geographical background
to the Irish Question.Short bibliography.

FOSTER, John Wilson : <u>Forces & themes in Ulster fiction</u> .
1974. Dublin / New-York. Gill & Macmillan. p. 299

A critical study of Ulster fiction from 1794 to the present
day. Valuable survey of the tensions, expressions, allegories,
and myths of the Ulster people. Short bibliography.

GLASSCOCK, E. R & BECKETT, J. C (editors) : Belfast. Origin & Growth
of an industrial city.
1967. London. BBC publications. 204 p.

Essential reading. Short bibliography.

GREAVES, Desmond : The Irish Crisis.
1972.London.Lawrence & Wishart. 222 p.

From the Partition of Ireland to the present day.The author
argues that a United Ireland is just as much in the interest
of the mass of the English people as the Irish.

HESLINGA, M. W : The Irish Border as a cultural divide.
1962. Assen. Van Gorcum / New-York. Humanities Press. 236 p
1971. Assen. Van Gorcum. (Second unrevised edition).

Foreword by Dr. E.E. Evans (see p.16).
Assessment of the historical prblem of the division of Ireland.
The author deals with Irish culture and traditions and conclu-
des that they are different North & South of the Border.
This analysis is also shared by Communists who name it as the
" Two nations theory ".It has been the subject of much contro-
versy in the past years. The Provisional IRA rejects it and
argues that Ulster Protestants are Irish not British.

See also : O'BRIEN,C.C : States of Ireland.(Page 41)
            WORKERS ASSOCIATION :One island,Two Nations.(P.126)

HEWITT, James (ed.) : Eye-witness to Ireland in revolt.
1974. Reading. Osprey Publishing. 178 p.

A reader of Irish rebellions from 1641 to 1916.

HILL, George : An historical account of the Plantation in Ulster at the
commencement of the 17th century. 1608 - 1620.
1877. Belfast.
1970. Shannon. Irish University Press.

Essential reading for detailed research.

HUTCHINSON, W.R : Tyrone Precinct : a History of the Plantation settlement of Dungannon & Mountjoy to modern times.
1951. Belfast. E.Mayne. 236 p.

Valuable bibliography for background reading and detailed work.

KEE, Robert : The Green Flag.
1972. London. Weidenfeld & Nicholson. 877 p.

A history of Irish nationalism from 1170 to 1923, detailed
from the end of the eighteenth century. Concerned particularly with Ireland's relationship with England.
Valuable introduction to the subject.

LYONS, F. S. L : <u>Ireland since the Famine</u>.
1971. London. Weidenfeld & Nicholson. 880 p.
1973. London. Fontana. (Revised edition).

The standard work on the period. The last chapter covers up
to the end of 1972. Extensive bibliography.
Essential reading.

McCAFFREY, Lawrence J : <u>The Irish Question 1800 / 1922</u>.
1968. University of Kentucky Press. Lexington. 202 p.

MACDONAGH, Oliver : <u>Ireland</u>.
1968. Englewood Cliffs. New Jersey. Prentice-Hall. 146 p.

From the Act of Union with Great Britain to 1968.

MACARDLE, Dorothy : <u>The Irish Republic : A chronicle of the Anglo-Irish</u>
<u>Conflict</u>.
1937. London. Gollancz.
1968. London. Corgi Books (5th edition). 989 p.

A detailed history of the period 1912 - 1925. Considered as
the standard work despite a strong republican bias. The preface was written by Eamon De Valera.
Short bibliography and useful biographical notes.

MANNING, Maurice : <u>Irish Political Parties. An Introduction</u>.
1972. Dublin. Gill & Macmillan. 120 p.

Useful introduction to the subject. Bibliography.

SENIOR, Hereward : <u>Orangeism in Ireland and Britain. 1795 - 1836</u>.
1966. London. Routledge & Kegan. / New-York. Hillary. 314 p.

The standard work. Essential reading for detailed research.
Bibliography.

SHEARMAN, Hugh : <u>Northern Ireland : 1921 - 1971</u>.
1971. Belfast. HMSO.

An official history published for the 50th anniversary of the
state. Pictorial and narrative.

STRAUSS, Emile : <u>Irish Nationalism & British Democracy</u>.
1951. London. Methuen. 307 p.

A Marxist analysis of the Irish Question. The main body of the
work is devoted to an analysis of the forces which moulded
Irish & English history during the period 1801 - 1921. The
author also shows in what way Irish problems affected the important developments of English history during the last century and a half.

WILSON, Harold : <u>The Labour Government. 1964 - 1970</u>.
1971. London. Weidenfeld and Nicholson.

See relevant passages about Ulster. Harold Wilson was Prime
Minister of Great Britain from 1966 to 1970 and then from
1974.

<u>FOR MEMBERS OF PARLIAMENT</u> :
   n.d (c.1935). Belfast. Author & sponsor unknow, marked " Con-
   fidential ".

   Memorandum about the killings of Roman Catholics in Belfast
   in the riots of 1935.
   See also BOYD, Andrew in Relevant articles Section.

AKENSON, D. H : <u>Education & Enmity</u>.The control of schooling in Northern
   Ireland . 1920 - 1950 .
   1973. David & Charles. Newton Abott. p.287

   Entirely concerned with the problem of segregated schooling
   in Northern Ireland. It is important to note that after the
   Partition of Ireland the Unionist Government in Belfast,
   led by Craigavon, intended to have non-denominational schools.
   Extremists in the Unionist Party and the reluctance of the
   Roman Catholic Church put an end to a fair educational sys-
   tem in the Province.
   See also CONWAY, William in Pamphlets Section.

ARMOUR, W. A : <u>Armour of Ballymoney</u>.
   1934. London.

   Biography of a prominent Protestant Home Ruler.

ARTHUR,Paul : <u>The People's Democracy. 1968 - 1973</u> .
   1974. Belfast. Blackstaff Press. p. 159

   The first study of this student left-wing revolutionary group,
   founded at the beginning of the present crisis on October 11,
   1968 . The author was a member of the group since its foundation. People's Democracy was much similar to other European
   student movements but had from its emergence its distinctive
   style. One of its leaders, Michael Farrell is still very much
   involved in Northern Ireland politics (See Pamphlets section).
   Useful appendices on statement of policy & political programme.

AYEARST, Morley : <u>The Republic of Ireland</u>. Its government & politics.
   1970. New-York. University Press. p.241
   1971. London. University of London Press.

   From the nineteenth century to 1969. Useful chapter on " Politics since the Treaty ". Good introduction to the subject.
   Short but valuable glossary of Irish words and phrases.

BARRITT, Denis & CARTER, Charles : <u>The Northern Ireland Problem</u>.
   A study in group relations.
   1962. London. Oxford University Press. p.163
   1972. London / New-York . OUP. (second revised edition)p.176

The first sociological study of community conflict in Northern Ireland. It investigates social relations, discrimination, politics, religion, etc... The work has not been updated in the second edition but a new preface was added. Essential reading.

BARZILAY, David : The British Army in Ulster.
1973. Belfast. Century Services . p.254

The author, a journalist, sympathetically described the activities of the British Army in Northern Ireland from 1969 to 1973. He reviews the weapons of the IRA, the guns, the bombs and the booby traps, and the weapons that the Army used in reply, the CS gas, rubber bullets and armoured vehicles. He also explains how several military operations were mounted and planned.
Statistics and pictures were supplied by the Press Office of the Army.

BARZILAY, David & MURRAY, Michael : Four months in winter.
1972. Belfast. The Second Battalion Royal Regiment of Fusiliers. p. 93

A log book of the tour in Northern Ireland of the British Army Second Battalion Royal Regiment of Fusiliers. Useful insight of the work of the British Army in Ulster and especially in some districts of Belfast.

BIGGS-DAVIDSON, John : The Hand is Red.
1973. London. Johnson. p.202

The Red Hand is the emblem of Ulster.
A brief account of the story of Ulster from the earliest times to the present day by an English Roman Catholic MP who is a member of the Right Wing Conservative Monday Club.The author says that this work is not so much a history as an essay in the " de-mythologizing " of the interpretation of Irish history.

BLAKE, J. W : Northern Ireland in the Second World War.
1956. Belfast. HMSO.

Official history. Northern Ireland played an important part in the war on the European and Atlantic fronts.American troops were based there, whereas the Irish Free State had declared itself neutral.
In a speech in Belfast in 1945 General Eisenhower said :
" It was here in Northern Ireland that the American Army first began to concentrate for our share in the attack upon the citadel of continental Europe. From here started the long, hard march to Allied victory. Without Northern Ireland I do not see how the American Forces could have been concentrated to begin the invasion of Europe. If Ulster had not been a definite, co-operative part of the British Empire and had not been available for our use, I do not see how the build-up could have been carried out in England . "

20

BLAKE, R : <u>The unknown Prime Minister (Bonar Law)</u>.
1955. London.

As Leader of the Conservative Party, Bonar Law strongly sup-
ported the Ulstermen in the Irish crisis of 1912 - 1914 .

BLEAKELEY, David : <u>Peace in Ulster</u>.
1972. London & Oxford. Mowbrays. p. 132

The author, a member of the NILP and a former Minister of Community Relations in the Stormont Cabinet (from 24. 3. 1971
to 25. 9. 1971) , expresses optimism about the future in
Northern Ireland.

BLEAKELEY, David : <u>Brian Faulkner</u>.
1974. Mowbrays. London & Oxford. p. 204

A sympathetic portrait of the former Prime Minister of Nor-
thern Ireland (from 24. 3. 1971 to 24. 3. 1972) who be-
came Chief Executive of the Northern Ireland Assembly on
January 1st, 1974. He resigned on May 28, 1974 after the
Ulster Workers Council's strike.
See in Appendices several speeches from 1949 to 1974.

BOLAND, Kevin : <u>We won't stand (idly) by</u> .
1972. Dublin. Published by the author. p. 138.

The title is a quotation from one of John Lynch's speeches after the violence of August 1969 in Northern Ireland (See LYNCH p. 13) .
The author comes from a strong Republican background. His
father had founded the Fianna Fail political party with
Eamon De Valera. Kevin Boland was elected to the Irish
Parliament in 1957 and became Secretary of Fianna Fail
and Minister of Local Government. Following the eruption
of violence in 1969 in Ulster , the Prime Minister of
the Irish Republic, John Lynch, refused to intervene mili-
tarily in the North. Later he sacked two of his ministers
suspected to have been behind the illegal import of arms
for the Catholic minority in Northern Ireland (See also
MacINTYRE, Tom in this section). Kevin Boland resigned
in protest.
This book describes his republican view and philosophy,
aspiring for a united Ireland.

BOULTON, David : <u>The UVF. 1966 - 1973</u> .
1973. Dublin. Gill & MacMillan. p. 188

A British television journalist analyses the origins of Protestant extremism since 1966 and especially the " second "
Ulster Volunteer Force and the Ulster Defence Association
(UDA).
The UVF (second version) was banned by the Stormont parliament on June 28, 1966 and declared legal on April 4, 1974
by the Secretary of State for Northern Ireland, Merlyn Rees.

21

For the " first " Ulster Volunteer Force see STEWART, A. T .Q
in this section.
The UDA is a paramilitary organisation which appeared in the
streets of Belfast in September 1971 as a reaction to IRA
activities. In May 1972 it patrolled protestant districts
and towns and erected barricades. In May 1974 it largely
contributed to the success of the Ulster Workers Council's
strike by using the same methods. This organisation was at
no time outlawed.
Essential reading despite the absence of notes, references
and index .

BOWYER BELL, J : The Secret Army. History of the IRA. 1916 - 1970.
    1970. London. A.Blond. p.405

    The Secret Army. History of the IRA. 1916 - 1974.
    1974. Cambridge. (Mass.) MIT Press. p. 434

    The standard work on the subject.
    A very detailed history of the IRA by an American historian.
    The American edition is thoroughly updated and analyses in
    detail the military campaign of the Provisional IRA.
    Essential reading to understand the split in the movement
    in 1969 leading to the formation of the " Provisional " IRA
    and the " Official " IRA. The latter has a strong marxist
    philosophy and has declared a ceasefire on May 29, 1972.
    It is important to note that the political wings of these
    armies have also split : thus the Provisional Sinn Fein
    organisation is the political wing of the Provisional IRA.
    In most newspaper reports the Sinn Fein organisations are
    referred to their location in Dublin :
    Official Sinn Fein is also known as Gardiner St Sinn Fein.
    Provisional Sinn Fein is also knwon as Kevin St Sinn Fein.

    Extensive bibliography and notes.

BOYCE, D. G : Englishmen & Irish Troubles. British Public Opinion &
    the making of the Irish policy. 1918 - 1922.
    1972. London. J.Cape. p.253

    How very often the Irish Question was discretely kept out
    of British newspapers.
    Bibliography.

BOYD, Andrew : Holy war in Belfast.
    1969. Tralee. Anvil Books. p.204
    1970. Tralee. Anvil Books. (Second revised edition) p.220

    The author traces the long and episodic clashes of sectarian
    violence in Belfast since the nineteenth century until Sep-
    tember 1969.
    Essential reading.

BOYD, Andrew : The rise of the Irish trade unions. 1729 - 1970
    1972. Tralee. Anvil Books. p. 155

22

Few books have been written on the history of the trade unions
in Ireland and this is a short one showing that trade unions
existed in Ireland since the end of the eighteenth century.
It also examines the part played by the unions - North and
South - in the present crisis in Northern Ireland.
Short bibliography.

BOYD, Andrew : Brian Faulkner and the crisis of Ulster Unionism.
1972. Tralee . Anvil Books. p.144

The first biography of the former Northern Ireland Prime
Minister (from 24. 3. 1971 to 24. 3. 1972).
Informative but the author takes a partisan view against all
Unionists.

BRADY, Conor : Guardians of the Peace.
1974. Dublin. Gill & MacMillan. p.254

A history of the Irish police, the Garda Siochana, an unarmed
police force established in 1922 by the Government of the Irish
Free State.
There has been little work published about the police in the
North or the South of Ireland and this volume is extremely
useful.
See also HAZLETT in this section, and BREATHNACH on this page.

BRADY, Seamus : Arms & the men. Ireland in turmoil.
1971. Wicklow. Published by the author. p.216

The personal account of one of the men closely involved with
the propaganda machine of the Irish Republic following the
1969 riots in Northern Ireland. The Irish Government had made £175,000 available to help the northern community (the
Roman Catholic minority) - of which £75,000 for propaganda
purposes - Seamus Brady, a native of Londonderry, went to
Northern Ireland in autumn 1969 and produced a news-sheet called " The Voice of the North ".
See also MacINTYRE in this section.
There are no notes, references, bibliography and index.

BREATHNACH, Seamus : The Irish police.
1974. Dublin. Anvil Books. p.230

The author served several years in the Garda Siochana.
This is a brief history of the Irish police, from the ear-
liest times to the present day.
Notes, references and short bibliography.

BRIEN, Francis William (ed.) : Divided Ireland : the roots of the conflict; a study into the causes of disorders in Northern Ireland.
1971. Rockford. Rockford College Press. p.77

BROMAGE, Mary . C : De Valera & the march of a nation.
1956. London. Hutchinson. p.328
1967. London. Four Square. p.157

A biography of Eamon De Valera, the founder of modern Ireland, the man who severed the last connections with England and kept Ireland out of the war.
See also LONGFORD & O'NEILL in this section.

BUDGE, Ian & O'LEARY, Cornelius : Belfast : approach to crisis. A study of Belfast politics. 1613 - 1970 .
1973. London / New-York. Macmillan. 396 p.

Two academics analyse the growth of religious intolerance in the city and the riots of the nineteenth century. They explore the institutional background to Unionist dominance (ie. gerrymandering) and suggest that the explosion of present violence is linked to the very moderation of the former Prime Minister of Northern Ireland, Captain Terence O'Neill.
Valuable statistics.
Essential reading for detailed research.

BUSTEED, M. A : Northern Ireland.
1974. London. Oxford University Press. 48 p.
(Problem Regions of Europe Series)

This short work concentrates mainly on economic and regional problems. There are some overgeneralisations but it is useful as an introduction to the subject.
Bibliography.

CALLAGHAN, James : A house divided. The dilemna of Northern Ireland.
1973. London. Collins. 207 p.

Accounts of a former British Home Secretary dealing with Northern Ireland between 1969 and 1970 . Interesting details about the reform of the Royal Ulster Constabulary and the use of CS gas (See also STETLER in this section) . James Callaghan sent British troops in Northern Ireland on August 14, 1969 to quell riots in Londonderry & Belfast. The author concludes his work by saying that he hopes ultimately to see an Ireland united by consent.

CALVERT, Harry : Constitutional law in Northern Ireland.
1968. London & Belfast. Stevens & Sons.

Basic work on the subject.

CAMPBELL, T. J : Fifty years of Ulster. 1890 - 1940 .
1941. Belfast. The Irish News. 400 p.

A Roman Catholic lawyer and a one time editor of the Nationalist Belfast daily newspaper (founded in 1891) tells of the evolution of the Province. Invaluable details. Essential reading to understand the feelings of the Northern minority.

CARROLL, H. T : Ireland in the war years. 1939 - 1945 .
1974. Newton Abbot. David & Charles /New-York. Crane, Russack & Co. 190 p.

24

With the help of the British Cabinet Papers recently released, the author makes a thorough examination of the Republic of Ireland 's reason for " neutrality " during the last war. The policy of neutrality was officially adopted by the Irish Parliament on September 2, 1939. The author examines the British offer of Irish unity in 1940 and the American campaign to force De Valera to expel the Axis diplomats in 1944.
Bibliography.

CARSON, William . A : Ulster and the Irish Republic.
        n.d (c. 1956) Belfast. W.Cleland. 57 p.

        Foreword by David Gray, United States Minister to Eire 1940 - 1947 .
        The role played by Northern Ireland during the second world war and the reasons why the Province should stay within the United Kingdom.

CHUBB, Basil : The Government and politics of Ireland.
        1970. London / New-York. Oxford University Press. 364 p.
        1974. London / New-York. OUP. 364 p.

        Historical introduction by David Thornley.
        Standard work. Bibliography.
        See in Appendices : basic social & economic data ; the electorate & elections; tables of Ministers from 1919 to 1968 ; state-sponsored bodies in 1968 and the Dail (Irish Parliament) Electoral System as it stood in 1969.

CLARK, Wallace : Guns in Ulster.
        1967. Belfast. Northern Whig. 126 p.

        Foreword by Lord Brookeborough , former Northern Ireland Prime Minister (1943 - 1963).
        A Protestant member of the Ulster Special Constabulary (the B-Specials - See HEZLET in this section),created in 1920 & stood down on April 30, 1970 , tells the history of a district area from 1921 to 1966 and the organisation of its defence against republicans.

COOGAN, T. P : The IRA.
        1970. London. Pall Mall Press. 373 p.
        1971. London. Fontana. (second revised edition.) 446 p.

        The author is editor of the Dublin daily newspaper The Irish Press.
        A fairly detached history but less detailed than BOWYER BELL's work (See p.22 of this section). The revised edition takes up the story to June 1970.

CRAWFORD, F. H : Guns for Ulster .
        1947. Belfast. Graham & Heslip. 80 p.

        Short but informative account of the personal involvement of Major F.H. Crawford in gun-running to arm the Ulster Volunteer Force when Ulster Protestants threatened armed rebellion if

Home Rule had been introduced in Ireland.
See also STEWART, A.T.Q in this section.

CRONIN, Sean : <u>Ireland since the Treaty</u> . Fifty years after .
1971. Dublin. Irish Freedom Press. 96 p.

A Republican analysis by a former Chief of Staff of the IRA
(before the split) who is presently the American correspondent of the Dublin based newspaper <u>The Irish Times</u>.

CRONIN, Sean : <u>The McGarrity Papers</u> . Revelations of the Irish Revolutionary movement in Ireland & America. 1900 - 1940 .
1972. Tralee. Anvil Books. 214 p.

At the beginning of the century, Joseph McGarrity was an
important figure in the Irish revolutionary movement in America. He was born in Ulster, in County Tyrone, and had ar-
rived in America at the age of 16. He became a leading member of Clan-na-Gael and played an important part in the activities of the IRA in Ireland and in Great-Britain.
Valuable notes, references and glossary.

CROWE, W. Haughton : <u>Beyond the hills : an Ulster headmaster remembers</u>.
1971. Dundalk. Dundalgan Press. 239 p.

CROZIER, Brian & MOSS, Robert (editors) : <u>The Ulster debate</u> . Report
of a study group of the Institute for the study of Conflict.
1972. London / Toronto. Bodley Head. 160 p.

Five studies on Ulster before Direct Rule was imposed by Lon-
don in March 1972.
See also BECKETT, CATHERWOOD, CHALFONT, FITZGERALD, LYONS &
MOSS in Articles section.
See in Appendices : Essential data & an Ulster chronology .

CROZIER, Frank Percy : <u>Ireland for ever</u>.
1932. London. Cape. 301 p.
1971. Bath. Chivers. (new edition)

The biography of Captain F. P Crozier who was involved in the
gun-running for the UVF in 1913 - 1914.
See also CRAWFORD p.25 and STEWART, A.T.Q in this section.

DALY, Cahal. B : <u>Violence in Ireland and Christian conscience</u>.
The Bishop of Ardagh & Clonmacnois analyses & criticizes the
present conflict. He also proposes a christian solution in
this collection of statements and articles.

DE PAOR, Liam : <u>Divided Ulster</u>.
1970. Harmondsworth. Penguin Special. 208 p.
1971. Harmondsworth. Pelican Books. (revised edition). 250 p

A short history - one of the best - of Ulster from the plantation to the resignation of Major Chichester-Clark, Northern
Ireland Prime Minister (from 1. 5. 1969 to 20. 3. 1971) .
The author argues that the religious divisions of the Province have been used as an instrument of policy and have masked

serious economic and social problems.

DEVLIN, Bernadette : <u>The Price of my Soul</u>.
1969. London. A. Deutsch / New - York. Vintage Books. 206 p.

The autobiography of the youngest Member of Parliament in the
British House of Commons. The author was elected, when she
was 22 years old, on April 17, 1969 to a Westminster seat in
a by - election in Mid - Ulster. (She kept her seat until
the General Election of February 1974).
She took a leading part in the civil rights movement and demon-
strations.She soon became a world famous figure, " The Joan
of Arc " of the Irish Catholics, as most of the media used to
describe her. She belonged to a certain number of left -wing
parties and lately she joined the Irish Republican Socialist
Party formed in December 1974 following a slipt in the Official Sinn Fein Party.
Essential reading to understand the feelings of the minority
in the North.

DEWAR, M. W & BROWN, John &LONG, S. E : <u>Orangeism : a new historical
appreciation.</u>
1967. Belfast .Grand Orange Lodge of Ireland. 201 p.
1969. (Second edition).

A collection of three essays by members of the Orange Order.
1 - 1688 - 1691 : deals with the life and the background of
William III, Prince of Orange - Nassau &
King of Great Britain and Ireland, from
whom the Orange Order takes its name; and
with the events of the years 1688 - 1691
(Battle of the Boyne in 1690) which the
Orange Institution celebrates every year.
2 - 1795 - 1886 : deals with the eighteenth & the early nineteenth centuries in which much Orangeism
came into being. It covers the Battle of
the Diamond, the 1798 Rebellion and the
part played by the Orange Order in the
early years of the Union between Great
Britain and Ireland.
3 - 1886 - 1967 : deals with the part played by the Ulster
Loyalists & Orangemen in the late nineteen-
th century, and in the present century.It
analyses the maintenance of the Protestant
religion and the Act of Union during the
past hundred years by Orangemen.

Since the foundation of the state of Northern Ireland the
minority there has always accused the Orange Order to be the
backbone of the Ulster Unionist Party and very often at the
origin of sectarian riots. See also BOYD, Andrew : <u>Holy War</u>
in Belfast (P.22) and Ultach (P.124).

Essential reading to understand the point of view of Orangemen.

27

DILLON, Martin & LEHANE, Denis : <u>Political murder in Northern Ireland</u>.
1973. Harmondsworth. Penguin Special / Baltimore (Maryland)
318 p.

Two Belfast journalists investigate about 200 sectarian assassinations between 1972 & 1973. Gruesome details about the circumstances of the killings. They argue that most of the assassinations were carried out by Protestant extremists. In the
last chapter, the authors suggest that the British Army , working with undercover patrols , may have been responsible for
some murders (See also KITSON, Brigadier : <u>Low-Intensity
Operations</u>. in this section).
In December 1974, following a writ issued by Charles Harding-
Smith, a former UDA Chairman, the publishers withdrew the
book.
Essential reading to understand the fears of the two communities during this period . There is no index.

DOUGAN, Derek : <u>The sash he never wore</u> .
1972. London. Allison & Busby .
1974. London. Mayflower Books. (Second edition)

Autobiography of a successful footballer born in Protestant
working - class Belfast. The sash, of orange colour, is worn
by members of the Orange Order.

DUDLEY EDWARDS, Owen : <u>The sins of our fathers : roots of conflict in
Northern Ireland</u> .
1970. Dublin / London. Gill & Macmillan. 353 p.

A personal view of the troubles by a young Irish historian .
Not so much an academic study but rather a pamphlet and a
socialist essay.
No index or bibliography.

EDMONDS, Sean : <u>The gun, the law & the Irish people</u> . From 1912 to the
aftermath of the Arms Trial 1970 .
1971. Tralee. Anvil Books. 279 p.

A short history of modern Ireland by a former Republican, editor of the provincial newspaper <u>The Tipperary Star</u>.
The author raises the issue of physical force versus constitu-
tionalism in Irish politics and traces its course through the
very eventful period of the 20th century. Interesting details
on the recent years.
Index but no bibliography or references.

ELLIOT, R. S. P & HICKIE, John : <u>Ulster. A Case study of conflict theory</u>.
1971. London. Longman. 180 p.

Most fieldwork for this book was done in 1969. It examines the
Ulster situation as a case study in conflict theory. Interesting interviews with political leaders of all the different
groupings involved in the troubles. Discussion of the results.
Chapter 2 : <u>Background to the conflict in Ulster</u> is not always very accurate.

ERVINE, St John : <u>Craigavon Ulsterman</u> .
1949. London. Allen & Unwin. 676 p.

A well-know Ulster playwright, the author states in his pre-
face of this massive official biography that it is not a for-
mal biography and that he " expounds & interprets...the be-
liefs & political faith of Ulster Unionists, of whom I am one ".
Valuable material but rather uncritical.
James Craig, later Lord Craigavon, was at the head of the anti-
Home Rule campaign in Ulster. He later became Prime Minister
of Northern Ireland from 1921 to 1940 .
(See also STEWART, A.T.Q : <u>The Ulster Crisis</u> in this section)
No bibliography but full index.

FENNELL, Desmond (ed.) : <u>The changing face of Catholic Ireland</u>.
1968. Dublin / London. Geoffrey Chapman. 223 p.

A series of articles reprinted from the <u>Herder Correspondence</u>,
from September 1964 to January 1968 . They examine Irish Catholic history in the 20th century including the impact of the
Second Vatican Council.

FIELDS, Rona. M : <u>A society on the run</u>. A psychology of Northern Ireland.
1973. Harmondsworth. Penguin Education Books. 216 p.

The author, an American psychologist, argues that the British
Government is pursuing a policy of " psychological genocide "
in Northern Ireland. This book was badly produced and it was
later withdrawn from sale by the Publishers. The author claims
that it was because of censorship.
See especially a series of tests on the psycho-motor and personality function of 125 ex-internees of Long Kesh internment
camp.
Bibliography.
(See also MACGUFFIN,John : <u>Internment</u> & <u>The Guineapigs</u> in
this section)

FITZGERALD, Garret : <u>Towards a new Ireland</u> .
1972. London. Charles Knight . 190 p.
1973. Dublin. Gill & Macmillan . (second edition) 190 p.

The author is Minister for Foreign Affairs for the Republic
of Ireland since March 1973 and was previously economic spo-
kesman for the Fine Gael Party.
This work considers the past effects of partition in Ireland,
North & South . The author argues that both parts of Ireland
need to change before one can speak of a united Ireland.
Useful appendix comparaing social welfare provisions in Northern Ireland and the Republic of Ireland.
Essential reading.

FITZGIBBON, Constantine : <u>Red Hand</u> . The Ulster Colony .
1971. London. Michael Joseph. 367 p.

The author, an American born Irishman, argues that the Ulsterman is " a unique miniature society suffering from an emotio-

nal split personality ". The author covers the history of
Ulster since the Plantations of the seventeenth century to
the riots of Belfast in 1970. Extensive quotations from
more original works.
In Appendix D see the chapter written by Wallace CLARK (p.
25 in this section) explaining the position of the various
paramilitary organizations in recent years.
C.FITZGIBBON says that he " displays a very considerable
bias against Protestant extremists in the North ".
Index but no bibliography.

FLANAGAN, P : Ulster.
1970. London. Heineman.

A geographical survey.

FORESTER, Margery : Michael Collins. The Lost Leader.
1971. London. Sidwick & Jackson. 370 p.
1972. London. Sphere Books (Second edition).

The most recent and one of the best biographies of Michael
Collins. He was one of the Irish representatives sent to London to arrange a settlement in 1921 with the British Government. (See also : JONES, Thomas : Whitehall Diary, in this
section). He was assassinated in August 1922 by a group of
republicans, 8 months after becoming Chairman of the Irish
Free State Provisional Government.
Bibliography, glossary and index.

FRASER, Morris : Children in conflict.
1973. London. Secker & Warburg. 167 p.
1974. Harmondsworth. Pelican Books (Second edition).

A leading Belfast child psychiatrist examines the human suffering & psychiatric effects of the "troubles" on children
in Northern Ireland. Dr Fraser argues that primary-school
integration would contribute more than any other single factor to the prospect of peace in Ulster, and draws the con-
clusion that while religious and racial segregation of schoolchildren exists, community strife will continue.
Extensive bibliography but no index.
(See also FIELDS, Rona : A society on the run. p.29 in this
section).
Essential reading.
(See also FRASER, M in Articles Section).

GALLAGHER, Frank : The Indivisible Island. The story of the partition
of Ireland.
1957. London. Gollancz. 316 p.

The origin, development & execution of Partition. The work
covers also the administration of Northern Ireland in all its
aspects : central and local government, police, electoral system, etc...
Bibliography & index.
Essential reading despite its partisan view.

(See also LONGFORD : <u>Peace by Ordeal</u> in this section)

GRAY, Tony : <u>The Orange Order.</u>
1972. London.Toronto. Bodley Head. 292 p.

A short history of this Protestant organization from its foundation in 1795 to the present day . The author analyses this
semi-secret society, organized in Lodges in the Masonic style
and sworn to uphold the Protestant ascendancy. He also examines the Orange Order in Canada, Australia, New - Zealand , England, Scotland and Africa.
Valuable introduction to the subject, short bibliography and
index.
See also DEWAR & LONG & BROWN : <u>Orangeism : a new historical</u>
<u>appreciation</u> . page 27 of this section and SENIOR : <u>Orangeism</u>
<u>in Ireland & Britain</u> .<u>1795 - 1836</u> . page 18 in General Works
section.

GREAVES, C. Desmond : <u>The life and times of James Connolly.</u>
1961. London / New - York. Lawrence & Wishart. 448 p.
1972. London / New - York. Lawrence & Wishart. 448 p. (second
edition)

The author is editor of <u>the Irish Democrat</u> newspaper published in London and a member of the British Communist Party.
James Connolly was born in Edinburgh in 1868 of Irish parents.
In 1895 he moved to Ireland and became a leading member of
the Irish Trade Union & Socialist movements. He was executed
by the British Army after the Easter Rising of 1916 in Dublin
in which he took a leading role. He also spent seven years
in the U.S.A where he worked with Daniel DE Leon's Socialist
Labor Party. Today there are a certain number of political
associations in Ireland following his analysis of the Irish
question.
Bibliography & index.
Essential reading, considered as the standard work on the subject but see also LEVENSON, Samuel : <u>James Connolly. A biogra-</u>
<u>phy.</u> in this section .

GWYNN, Denis. R : <u>The history of Partition : 1912 - 1925</u> .
1950. Dublin. Browne & Nolan.

How Ireland was partitioned. The author was a journalist and
historian who became Research Professor of Modern Irish History at University College, Cork from 1946 to 1963. He was
a strong anti-partitionist.
See also GALLAGHER : <u>The Indivisible Island</u> page 30 in this
section and LONGFORD : <u>Peace by Ordeal</u> in this section too .

HARBINSON, John F.: <u>The Ulster Unionist Party. 1882 - 1973</u> .
1973. Belfast. Blackstaff Press. 252 p.

One of the first studies of the Ulster Unionist Party, the majority party since the foundation of Northern Ireland. Valuable background information.
Useful Appendices : biographical notes on Ulster Unionist Se-
nators at Stormont Parliament from 1921 to 1969 ; biographi-

cal notes on Unionist Members of Parliament at both Stormont
and Westminster since the first sitting of the Northern Ireland Parliament in 1921 ; distribution of seats in Northern
Parliaments since 1921 to 1969 ; and list of minor Unionist
parties.
Short bibliography, notes , references and index.
See also BUCKLAND, Patrick page 16 in General Works Section.

HARBINSON, Robert : No Surrender: an Ulster Childhood .
1960. London.

The author used also the pseudonym BRYANS, Robin.
Autobiography of a popular Protestant Ulster writer born in
1928. Valuable descriptions of his childhood in the Protestant working-class Sandy Row area of Belfast and of his
work in the Belfast shipyards as a young man.

HARRIS, Rosemary : Prejudice & Tolerance in Ulster.
1972. Manchester. University Press / Totowa (N.J). Rowman &
Littlefield. 234 p.

Demographic & sociological research conducted in 1952 - 1953
in Ballybeg, a pseudonym for a small town close to the Northern Ireland Border with the Republic.A study in depth of
the nature of prejudice in Ulster.
Index and short bibliography.
Essential background reading.

HARRISON, Henry : Ireland & the British Empire 1937 . Conflict or Col-
laboration ?
1937. London. Robert Hall.

A plea for reconciliation of the United Kingdom and the Irish
Free State in view of the danger of a European war. The author,
an Irish nationalist, examines the role of the minority in
Northern Ireland, its lack of power to have its grievances
remedied and the Civil Authorities Act 1922 (The Special
Powers Act).
See also CARROLL,H. T : Ireland in the war years , page 24
in this section and NATIONAL COUNCIL FOR CIVIL LIBERTIES
in the Pamphlets section.

HARRISON, Henry : Ulster & the British Empire 1939 . Help or hindrance ?
1939. London. Robert Hall. 231 p.

The author describes the Anglo-Irish situation and what has
led to it. He asks the question : Is Britain sincere in her
proposed policy of Anglo-Irish appeasement ?
Valuable statistics prepared by the Intelligence Branch of
the financial British weekly The Economist .
Short index and no bibliography.

HASTINGS, Max : Ulster 1969. The fight for Civil Rights in Northern Ireland.
1970. London. Gollancz. 203 p.

Barricades in Belfast.
1970. New - York. Taninger. 203 p.

(This is the same work published under two different titles).
Solid work by an English journalist who deals mainly with
the early civil rights movement in Northern Ireland , from
1963 to 1969 .
Essential reading despite the lack of index , notes and bibliography.

HEALY, T. M : The great fraud of Ulster .
1917. Dublin. Gill & Macmillan (published under the title
Stolen Waters) 512 p.
1971. Tralee. Anvil Books. (abridged edition) 154 p.

Foreword by Dennis Kennedy, a journalist of the Irish Times ,
who reported extensively on devlopments in Northern Ireland
since the civil rights campaign.
The author was a supporter of the Home Rule campaign and
toured America with Parnell. Later he became Governor General of the Irish Free State in 1922. He died in 1931.
Healy retraces the history of Sir Arthur Chichester who was
the chief architect of the Plantation of Ulster and Lord De-
puty of Ireland from 1604 until his removal in 1615. He was
the founder of a landed family which held on to political
influence in Northern Ireland to the present period. James
Chichester-Clark, former Northern Ireland Prime Minister
(1969 - 1971) belongs to this family.
In the introduction Dennis Kennedy examines the case of
Lough Neagh fishermen who lost a court case against the 6th
Marquess of Donegall, who had the exclusive rights over eel
fishing by virtue of a grant made in 1661.
See also FARRELL, Michael : The great eel robbery . in the
Pamphlets section.

HEZLET, Sir Arthur : The B - Specials . A history of the Ulster Special
Constabulary.
1972. London. Tom Stacey . 267 p.
1973. London. Pan Books. (second edition)

The first complete history of this police force since its creation to its disbandment in April 1970. The author examines its
organization, local activity and political background. Short
bibliography and index.
Essential reading .
See also the HUNT REPORT (page 6 in the Official Publications
Section) and BOWYER BELL: The Secret Army (page 22 in this
section) and COOGAN : The IRA (page 25 in this section) and
CLARK : Guns in Ulster (also page 25) .

HOLT, Edgar : Protest in Arms. The Irish troubles 1916 - 1923.
1960. London. Putnam. 328 p.

Good survey of the period, written in a popular style . Good
introduction to the subject. Bibliography and index.

HYDE, H. Montgomery : <u>Life of Lord Carson</u> .
     1953. London. Heinemann. 515 p.
     1974. London. Constable (second edition with new preface)

     A useful biography of this famous lawyer (see the chapter
     concerning Oscar Wilde's trial) who turned politician.
     During the British Liberal Government of 1905 - 1915 Carson
     led the British Protestant resistance to Home Rule and in
     1911 he set up an Ulster Unionist Council, which prepared a
     draft constitution for Ulster. In 1912 he organized a volun-
     teer force of 80,000 men, a 'private army' pledged to resist
     Home Rule.
     Extensive bibliography & index. Essential reading.
     See also :
     MARJORIBANKS & COLVIN: <u>Life of Lord Carson</u> (in this section)
     STEWART, A.T.Q : <u>The Ulster Crisis</u>.(in this section)

IRELAND, Denis : <u>From the Irish shore : notes on my life & times</u>.
     1936. London. Rich & Cowan. 244 p.

     An autobiography.
     The son of a linen manufacturer & merchant, the author born
     in 1894, was an influential Ulsterman. A Liberal - Nationalist
     he was the founder & President of the Ulster Union Club, an
     association of nationally minded Northern Protestants. He sat
     in the Irish Senate (in Dublin) from 1948 to 1951 as a Pro-
     testant member from Belfast. He was also at the time the Irish
     representative at the Council of Europe at Strasbourg. He died
     in 1974.

IRELAND, Denis : <u>From the Jungle of Belfast. Footnotes to history 1904 -
     1972</u> .
     1973. Belfast. Blackstaff Press. 175 p.

     The second part of his autobiography. It includes reflexions
     on the latest " troubles " in Belfast (see part VIII : Whi-
     le the bombs blew up Belfast).

ISLES, K. S & CUTHBERT, N : <u>An Economic survey of Northern Ireland.</u>
     1957. Belfast. HMSO. 647 p.

     Valuable work for reference material. This report provides
     an independent study of the economy of Northern Ireland on
     the basis of academic research.

JAMIESON, John : <u>The history of the Royal Belfast Academical Institu-
     tion.</u>
     1959. Belfast.

     The history of one of the leading Belfast public schools .

JONES, Thomas : <u>WHITEHALL DIARY : Vol III : Ireland 1918 - 1925</u> .
     edited by Keith Middlemass.
     1971. London / New - York . Oxford University Press .

     Thomas Jones was assistant Secretary to the British Prime

Minister Lloyd George. This last volume of the diaries kept
by Jones during his 15 years in Whitehall deals exclusively
with Irish affairs from 1918 to 1925. There are accurate notes about the Partition of 1920, the Truce, the Treaty negotiations and the Boundary Commission.
Notes, references and index.
Essential reading for detailed research.
See also : <u>REPORT OF THE IRISH BOUNDARY COMMISSION.1925</u>
(page 3 in Bibliographies & Reference works)

KELLY, Henry : <u>How Stormont fell</u>.
1972. Dublin. Gill & Macmillan. 150 p.

The former Northern editor of <u>the Irish Times</u> newspaper
analyses the last year of the Stormont Parliament (from
20. 3. 1971 to 24. 3. 1972) , from the appointment of
Brian Faulkner as Prime Minister to the last sitting of
the Stormont Parliament after it had been prorogued by the
British Government headed by the Conservative Prime Minister , Edward Heath.
Essential reading despite the lack of references and index.

KELLY, Capt. James : <u>Orders from the Captain</u>.
1971. Dublin . Published by the author. 246 p.

Former Irish Army Intelligence Captain tells his part in what
became known as the Arms Conspiracy in the Republic of Ireland in 1970.
Short chronology, some references but no index.
See also : BRADY, <u>Seamus :Arms & the men</u>. (page 23 in this
                section)
          McINTYRE, Thomas : <u>Through the Bridewell Gate</u> :
          <u>A Diary of the Dublin Arms Trial.</u> (in this
          section).

KIELY, Benedict : <u>Counties of Contention : A study of the origins and</u>
          <u>implications of the partition of Ireland</u>.
1945. Cork.

KENNA, G. B : <u>Facts & figures of the Belfast Pogrom 1920 - 1922</u> .
1922. Dublin. The O'Connell Publishing Co. 213 p.

From July 1920 to June 1922 455 persons were killed in the
rioting preceding and following the opening of the Stormont
Parliament on June 23 , 1921 by King George V . The author
accuses the Loyalists (ie.Protestants) of being responsi-
ble for the sectarian rioting.
Extensive quotations from newspapers . Index & references.
Essential reading.
See also : BOYD, Andrew : <u>Holy War in Belfast</u>. (page 22 in
                this section)
          ULTACH : <u>The Orange Terror</u> (in Pamphlets Section).

KITSON, Brigadier Frank : <u>Low - Intensity Operations</u>. Subversion, Insurgency & Peacekeeping.
1971. London. Faber & Faber. 208 p.

The author, a British Army expert of counter - insurgency ,
served two years in Northern Ireland with 39th Airportable
Brigade before writing this work.
He advocates the use of guerilla tactics by regular armies
to fight guerilla movements. The IRA & The NICRA have , at
several times, stated that the British Army in Ulster was
using undercover agents to carry out murders. References
to these " assassination squads " are also made in DILLON &
LEHANE : <u>Political murder in Northern Ireland</u> - Chap. 15 :
The killers : The British Army (See page 28 in this section).
Bibliography & index.

LAWRENCE, R. J : <u>The Government of Northern Ireland : Public Finance &
Public Services. 1921 - 1964 </u>.
1965. London / New - York. Oxford University Press. 198 p.

Problems of the new state and analysis of its origins & powers. Detailed studies of public services. In the last chapter the author reviews Northern Ireland 's experience and
considers whether devolution would be desirable and practi-
cable in Great Britain.
Notes & References & Index.
Essential reading for detailed research.

LEVENSON, Samuel : <u>James Connolly</u> - A biography.
1973. London. Martin O' Keefe.

The latest biography.
Bibliography & Index.
See also GREAVES, C.D : <u>The life & times of James Connolly</u>.
(page 31 of this section)

LIMPKIN, Clive : <u>The Battle of the Bogside</u>.
1972. Harmondsworth. Penguin Books. 172 p.

Press photographer records in pictures life in Londonderry
from 1969 to 1972.

LLOYD GEORGE, David : <u>War memoirs</u> .
1933 - 1936 . London. 6 vols.

As British Prime Minister he achieved a settlement of the Irish
problem when he signed with Michael Collins & Arthur Griffith
the Anglo-Irish Treaty on December 6, 1921. It gave Southern
Ireland dominion status.
Essential reading for detailed research.

LONGFORD, Lord (Pakenham, Frank) : <u>Peace by ordeal. The negotiation of
the Anglo-Irish Treaty 1921</u>.
1935. London. Cape.
1972. London. Sidgwick & Jackson (new edition with new preface
ce) 318 p.

The standard work. A detailed and valuable account with valuable documentary appendices of the Anglo-Irish Treaty which was later denounced by Eamon De Valera.
Notes, references, chronology and index.

LONGFORD, Earl of & O'NEILL, Thomas : <u>Eamon De Valera</u> .
        1970. London. Hutchinson. 499 p.
        1974. London. Arrow Books. 499 p.

        Official biography of the founder of modern Ireland. The authors make extensive use of the former President's private papers. In the later part of his life Eamon De Valera made little public reference to the situation in Northern Ireland.
        Notes, references and index.

McCANN, Eamonn : <u>War and an Irish town</u>.
        1974. Harmondsworth. Penguin Special. 256 p.

        In 1968 the author played a leading part in the early days of the civil rights campaign in Londonderry which are described in this work. In the autobiographical part he tells about his childhood and education as a Roman Catholic living in the " ghetto " of the Bogside. In this district, a poor Roman Catholic one, with high unemployment, took place most of the rioting in August 1969 . At one stage during the fighting with the RUC, the area was declared a " republic " and called " Free Derry ". In the second part of his work, the author gives a marxist analysis of the Irish question. Essential reading despite the lack of notes, references & index.

McDOWELL, R. B : <u>The Irish Convention. 1917 - 1918</u>.
        1970. London / Toronto. Routledge & Kegan Paul. 240 p.

        Following the Easter Rising the British Government tried to solve the Irish Question by convening a conference. It failed and in 1919 Sinn Fein representatives declared independence by meeting as Dail Eireann. The author examines the work of the Convention.
        See in appendix the list of members of the Convention.
        Essential reading for detailed research. Bibliography & index.

McIVOR, John A :<u>Popular education in the Irish Presbyterian Church</u>.
        1969. Dublin. Sceptre Publishers.

McNEILL, Ronald (Lord Cushendum) : <u>Ulster's stand for Union</u>.
        1922. London.

        The author was a Unionist MP at Westminster. He was also a member of the secret Provisional Government set up by Edward Carson in Northern Ireland in 1914 and ready to take over if the Home Rule Bill had been passed at Westminster. Some interesting details about the negotiations over the Partition of Ireland.

See also STEWART, A.T.Q : <u>The Ulster Crisis</u> (in this section)

MacGUFFIN, John : <u>Internment</u> !
1973. Tralee. Anvil Books. 228 p.

The history of internment in Ireland (North & South) since
the beginning of the twentieth century to 1972. The author
was interned on August 9, 1971 - when internment was introduced in Northern Ireland by the British Government - and then
released.
Extensive notes, references and bibliography. Index.
Essential reading.
See also :-<u>THE COMPTON REPORT</u> & <u>THE PARKER REPORT</u>.(Page 8
   in the Official Publications Section)

   -Campaign for Social Justice in Northern Ireland :
   <u>The mailed fist.</u>

   -Paul, Fr. Denis & Murray, Fr. Raymond :
   <u>British Army and Special Branch RUC Brutalities.</u>
   <u>Dec.1971 - Feb.1972.</u>

   <u>Whitelaw's Tribunals : Long Kesh internment camp.</u>
   <u>Nov.1972 - Jan.1973.</u>

   <u>The iniquity of internment. Aug.9, 1971 - Aug.9,</u>
   <u>1974.</u>

   <u>The Hooded men. British Torture in Ireland. Aug.-</u>
   <u>Oct.1971.</u>

   -O'Tuathail, Seamus : <u>They came in the morning.</u>
   <u>Internment. Monday August 9, 1971.</u>

   (All titles mentioned above are in the Pamphlets
   Section).

   -<u>HIBERNIA</u> : <u>1971 - Internment - 1974</u> (See articles
   Section).

MacGUFFIN, John : <u>The Guineapigs</u>.
1974. Harmondsworth. Penguin Special. 188 p.

The author describes the use by the British Army of modern
" torture " techniques (System of Sensory Deprivation) in
Northern Ireland following the introduction of internment.He
also shows how the authorities later tried to cover these in-
terrogations.
References & Notes but no index.
See also all the titles mentioned above.

MacINTYRE, Thomas : <u>Through the Bridewell Gate. A diary of the Dublin</u>
<u>Arms Trial</u>.
1971. London. Faber & Faber. 219 p.

In September 1970 Charles Haughey, Minister of Finance in the
Irish Cabinet, and three other persons were charged with conspiracy to import arms & ammunition into Eire illegally in Apr-

il 1970. The trial ended in October 1970 with all four defendants found not guilty. Since then Charles Haughey has returned to the Fianna Fail Party and is a strong contender for its leadership.
This work gives a fair account of the trial but cannot be as detailed as newspaper reports of the time (see especially The Irish Times).
Index and appendices.
See also : BRADY, Seamus : Arms & the men (page 23 in this
                       section)
          KELLY, Capt, James : Orders from the Captain.
          (Page 35 in this section).

McGUIRE, Maria : To take arms. A year in the Provisional IRA.
        1973. London. Macmillan. 159 p.
        1973. London. Quartet Books (second edition) 154 p.

        Middle-class Dublin student tells her involvement and shows
        how the Provisional campaign is waged. Useful for informa-
        tions on Sean MacStiofain (former Chief of Staff) and Da-
        vid O'Connell (probably the present Chief of Staff).
        Essential reading despite the lack of notes, references and
        index.

MANHATTAN, Avro : Religious terror in Ireland .
        1969. London. Paravision Publications.
        1970. London. Paravision Publications (revised edition) 221p

        According to the author " the cause of all evil is the Roman
        Catholic Church ", and his analysis of the present conflict
        is rather partisan.
        Notes but no index.

MANSERGH, Nicolas : The Government of Northern Ireland.
        1936. London. Allen. 335 p.

        The standard work. It considers the original nature of the
        government of Northern Ireland in the United Kingdom and
        judges the values of devolution as a method of government.

MANSERGH, Nicolas : The Irish Question. 1840 - 1921 . A commentary on
        Anglo-Irish relations and on social and political forces in
        Ireland in the Age of Reform and Revolution.
        1965 / 1968. London. Allen & Unwin. 316 p.

        A revised edition of Ireland in the age of reform and revolu-
        tion. (published in 1940).

        The standard work on the subject. Useful for studying the ef-
        fects of social and political forces on Anglo-Irish relations.
        Bibliography, notes , references and index.
        See also : MANSERGH, Nicolas :The Government of Ireland Act
                  1920 : its origins & purposes . (See Page 81 in
                  Articles Section).

MANSERGH, Nicolas : <u>Irish Free State : its government and politics</u>.
1934. London. Allen.

Standard work. Useful for the history of the early state and
its position regarding the Partition.
Bibliography, notes, references and index.
See also O'SULLIVAN,DONAL : <u>The Irish Free State and its
Senate.</u> (in this section).

MARJORIBANKS, Edward & COLVIN, Ian : <u>Life of Lord Carson</u>.
1932 - 1934 . London. Gollancz. 3 vols.

Standard work and official biography.
In 1910 Edward Carson assumed the leadership of the Ulster
Unionist Party in the Westminster House of Commons. He led
the British Protestant resistance to Home Rule and in 1912
he organized a volunteer force of 80,000 men pledged to re-
sist Home Rule. Later he became a member of the British
War Cabinet.
Bibliography, notes, references and index.

MARRINAN, Patrick : <u>Paisley: Man of wrath</u> .
1973. Tralee. Anvil Books. 260 p.

The first biography of the Reverend Ian Paisley, written by
a Catholic barrister . The Reverend Ian Paisley is the Mode-
rator of the Free Presbyterian Church of Ulster since 1946
and Minister of the Martyr Memorial Free Presbyterian Church
in Belfast since the same date.
He was successively elected Member of Parliament for the
Northern Ireland Parliament on April 17, 1970 and for the
Westminster Parliament on June 19, 1970.
He is the chairman of the Democratic Unionist Party launched
officially on October 30, 1971 and has taken a hard line position in the present situation in Ulster.
The author argues that the Reverend Ian Paisley split the mo-
nolithic face of Ulster Unionism.
Essential reading, but no bibliography . There is a short chro-
nology (not always accurate) and an index.
See also : DUDLEY EDWARDS, Owen : <u>A look at the Reverend Ian
Paisley.</u> (in the Articles section).

MOODY, T. W : <u>The Ulster Question. 1603 - 1973</u> .
1974. Cork. Mercier Press. 134 p.

Revised & extended version of a paper read in Dublin by a leading Irish historian. A concise handbook of the Ulster Question from Gaelic times to June 1973.
Useful bibliography & appendices, including the Sunningdale
agreement signed on December 9, 1973 by the Prime Ministers
of the Republic of Ireland and of Great Britain and the Chief
Executive designate of the Northern Ireland Assembly (See
also <u>Sunningdale Agreement</u> , page 11 in the Official Publications Section).
Essential reading.

MOODY, T. W & BECKETT, J. C : <u>The Queen's University. 1845 - 1949.</u>
<u>The History of a University.</u>
1959. London. Faber & Faber. 2 vols.

The standard work on the history of the university of Belfast.
Maps, plans & illustrations.

MOODY, T. W & BECKETT, J. C : <u>Ulster since 1800 : a political & eco-</u>
<u>nomic survey.</u>
1954. London. BBC Publications. 133 p.

<u>Ulster since 1800 : a social survey.</u> (Second series)
1957. London. BBC publications. 240 p.

A series of lectures first broadcast on BBC Northern Ireland radio in 1954, 1956 & 1957.

Essential reading, bibliography but no index.

See also RELEVANT CHAPTERS Section.

NARAIN, B. J : <u>Public law in Northern Ireland.</u>
1973. Belfast. Appletree Press. 156 p.

A discussion about future alternative settlements for Northern
Ireland from the basis of public law.

Notes, references but no index.

NEILL, D. G (ed.) : <u>Devolution of Government. The experiment in Northern</u>
<u>Ireland.</u>
1953. London. 99 p.

Collection of papers on different aspects of the achievements
of the Northern Ireland Parliament.

O'BRIEN, Conor Cruise : <u>States of Ireland.</u>
1972. London. Hutchinson.
1974. London. Panther Books (Revised edition) 327 p.

The author, a Labour member of the Irish Parliament and a
Minister in the Irish Cabinet since March 1973, examines the
complex Irish situation from the fall of Parnell to mid-April
1974. Part history,part autobiography,part political analysis,
it is one of the best and most interesting contributions to
the settlement of the Irish Question.
Conor Cruise O'Brien sees the future as either the defeat of
the IRA or a massive civil war in the North. In the latter
case the United Nations would intervene and there would be
a new Partition and a new Border.

As member of the Cosgrave Cabinet, C.C.O'Brien has been responsible for much of the policy of the Irish Government regarding Northern Ireland.

Notes, references, index but no bibliography.

Essential reading.

O'CONNELL, T. J : <u>History of the Irish National Teachers Organisation.</u>
<u>1868 - 1968 . 100 years of progress.</u>
1969. Dublin. Into.

O'CONNOR, Kevin : <u>The Irish in Britain.</u>
1972. London. Sidwick & Jackson. 188 p.
1974. Dublin. Gill & MacMillan (revised edition) 160 p.

A social history of Irish immigration to Britain . More than
400,000 Irish came there between 1950 & 1960 alone. The au-
thor deals with the period before the Union of Great Britain
& Ireland in 1800 to the present day.
Emigration has always been an important factor in Northern
Ireland's economy.

O'FARRELL, Patrick : <u>Ireland's English Question</u> . Anglo-Irish relations
1534 - 1970.
1971. London. Batsford. 336 p.

A re-interpretation of Anglo-Irish history seeking to explain
why successive British Governments failed to solve the Irish
Question especially in the nineteenth and twentieth centuries.
The author argues that the problem has been political but his-
torical and religious, a question of idendity.
Bibliography & Index.

O'NEILL, Terence (Lord of the Maine) : <u>Ulster at the crossroads.</u>
1969. London. Faber & Faber . 201 p.

Terence O'Neill was Prime Minister of Northern Ireland from
1963 to 1969 . He resigned in April 1969 after failing to introduce a number of reforms overdue and wanted by the minority.
This work is a collection of speeches from 1964 to 1969 .
The introduction by John Cole, assistant editor of the
<u>Guardian</u> , sets the scene and in a few pages manages to
explain the rather byzantine politics of Ulster.

O'NEILL, Terence : <u>The Autobiography of Terence O'Neill . Prime Minis-</u>
<u>ter Of Northern Ireland. 1963 - 1969.</u>
1972. London. Rupert Hart-Davis. 160 p.

An important document but little original informations and a
lot of superfluous anecdotes.
Essential reading to understand what O'Neill wanted to achie-
ve in Northern Ireland and his style of Unionism.
Index but no notes or bibliography.

O'SULLIVAN, Donal : <u>The Irish Free State & its Senate.</u> A study in contemporary politics.
1940. London. Faber & Faber. 666 p.

The standard work on the subject. See references to Northern
Ireland in this study of the working of the Irish Senate by
its Clerk. It covers the political history of the Irish Free
State from 1922 to 1939.
Essential reading for detailed research work.

See also MANSERGH, Nicolas : <u>The Irish Free State : its government and politics.</u> (page 40 in this section).

O'SULLIVAN, P. Michael : <u>Patriot Graves. Resistance in Ireland.</u>
1972. Chicago. Follett Publishing. 255 p.

Photographs and interviews of the Provisional IRA in Ireland
(North & South) during the present crisis by an American
journalist. Lengthy interviews of the leaders of the movement : Joe Cahill, Sean MacStiofain and David O'Connell.
Essential reading.

RIDDELL, Patrick : <u>Fires over Ulster.</u>
1970. London. Hamish Hamilton. 208 p.

A Unionist point of view of the 1968 - 1969 troubles by a well
known Northern journalist.

RIDDELL, Patrick : <u>The Irish - Are they real</u> ?
1972. London. Hamish Hamilton. 228 p.

Harsh & witty analysis of the Irish character.

ROSE, Richard : <u>Governing without consensus.</u> An Irish perspective.
1971. London. Faber & Faber . 567 p.

The standard work on the subject.
A major academic survey undertaken in 1965 and completed in
1970 by an American professor. The Northern Ireland problem
is introduced as one common to all Anglo-American societies,
and specially significant for the United Kingdom. The view
of the people of Northern Ireland are carefully presented by
a survey of public opinion undertaken just before violence
erupted in the streets. The appendix contains the full Loyal-
ty questionnaire and percentage responses.
Bibliography in footnotes, index.
Essential reading.
See also ROSE, Richard in Articles Section.
          WHYTE, John : <u>Governing without consensus.A criti-
          que.</u> (in Pamphlets Section).

SHEARMAN, Hugh : <u>Not an inch : A study of Northern Ireland & Lord Craigavon.</u>
1943. London. Faber & Faber. 184 p.

A popular biography.
See also ERVINE, St John : <u>Craigavon Ulsterman.</u>(page 29 in
          this section).

SHEARMAN, Hugh : <u>Anglo-Irish relations.</u>
1948. London. Faber & Faber.

An account of the historical relations between England & Ireland from the earliest times to 1948.

SHEEHY, Michael : <u>Divided we stand : a study of Partition</u>.
    1955. London. Faber & Faber. 104 p.

    A useful essay on Irish mentality on both sides of the Border
    by a young Catholic from the Republic of Ireland.

STETLER, Russell : <u>The Battle of the Bogside</u>. The politics of violence
    1970. London. Sheed and Ward. 213 p.

    A member of a team of scientists which visited Londonderry to
    study the effects of CS gas used there by the RUC in the riots
    of August 1969. Description of " The battle of the Bogside ".
    Brief social and economic background to the events leading to
    the barricades.
    Short bibliography, notes but no index.
    In Appendix valuable & lengthy chapter on " The development
    and use of CS gas " with bibliography.
    See also : DEVLIN, Bernadette : <u>The Price of my Soul</u>. (page
        27 in this section).
        McCANN, Eamonn : <u>War and an Irish Town</u>. (page 37
        in this section).

STEWART, A. T. Q : <u>The Ulster Crisis</u>.
    1967. London. Faber & Faber. 284 p.
    1972. London. Faber & Faber (second edition).

    The standard work on the period.
    It described the resistance to Home Rule in Ulster between the
    introduction of the Third Home Rule Bill in 1912 and the out-
    break of the Second World War. Extremely valuable for the his-
    tory of the Ulster Volunteer Force.
    Essential reading to understand contemporary problems in Uls-
    ter.
    Bibliography, notes and index.

    See also : CRAWFORD : <u>Guns for Ulster</u>. (page 25)
        CROZIER : <u>Ireland for ever</u>. (" 26)
        ERVINE : <u>Craigavon Ulsterman</u>.(" 29)
        HYDE : <u>Life of Lord Carson</u> .(" 34)
        McNEILL : <u>Ulster's stand for Union</u>.(page 37)

    (All titles mentioned above are in this section).

SUNDAY TIMES (Insight Team) : <u>ULSTER</u>.
    1972. Harmondsworth. Penguin Special. 311 p.
    1972. "   "   " (revised edition) 320 p
    1972. "   "   " (revised edition with
      new concluding chapter) 320 p.

    Revised and expanded version of two special articles on the
    Northern Ireland situation originally published in the <u>Sun-
    day Times</u> newspaper in November 1971.
    This work covers the period of the early civil rights campai-
    gn up to Easter 1972 after the introduction of Direct Rule
    (ie. the prorogation of the Northern Parliament by Westmins-
    ter). Although relying heavily on verbal evidence difficult
    to check, it is an important account of the recent period.

Maps, index but no bibliography.

SWEETMAN, Rosita : On our knees - Ireland 1972.
1972. London. Pan Books. 288 p.

24 interviews of prominent people in the North & South of Ireland. Each of them is preceded by background information.
See especially : Sean MacStiofain (one-time Chief of Staff
of the Provisional IRA)
Cathal Goulding (Chief of Staff of the
Official IRA)
The Reverend Martin Smyth (Grand Master
of the Orange Order)
Robert Cooper (a leader of the Alliance
Party of Northern Ireland, founded on April
21, 1970).

Valuable information despite the lack of references, notes or index.
The title is part of a quotation taken from a speech by the Dublin trade-union leader James Larkin : " The great are only great because we are on our knees - let us arise ! " (1912).

TARGET, G. W : Unholy smoke.
1969. London. Hodder & Stoughton. 127 p.

An Evangelical Protestant, formerly a Roman Catholic, the author describes what happens in Northern Ireland immediately after the beginning of the riots of August 1969.

US CONGRESS COMMITTEE ON FOREIGN AFFAIRS : Northern Ireland hearings before the subcommittee on Europe. 92nd Congress. Second Session.
1972. Washington. Government Printing Office. 639 p.

WALLACE, Martin : Drums & Guns - Revolution in Ulster.
1970. London. G.Chapman. 144 p.

One of the first works published after the crisis of August 1969. The author, a journalist who covered the rise of the civil rights movement, gives a brief but crisp historical background to the present troubles and discusses the British Government's intervention in Ulster and the future prospects. Essential reading despite the lack of notes, references and bibliography.

WALLACE, Martin : Northern Ireland - 50 years of self-government.
1971. Newton Abbot. David & Charles. 192 p.

A concise but clear survey of the achievements of the Northern Ireland Government since 1921. The author covers the political institutions, the local government, the judiciary, the Government of Ireland Act 1920, the relations with Westminster, education, health, etc...
Extensive quotations from major works.
Bibliography and Index.
Essential reading.

WARD, Alan. J : <u>Ireland and Anglo-American Relations. 1899 - 1921</u> .
1969. London. The London School of Economics & Political
Science / Weidenfeld & Nicholson. 291 p.

A comprehensive analysis of the part played by Ireland in the
conduct of Anglo-American relations and of the influence of
Irish immigrants (many of whom came from Ulster) over the
policies of the United States.
Bibliography & index.

WHYTE,J. H : <u>Church & State in Modern Ireland. 1923 - 1970</u> .
1971. Dublin. Gill & Macmillan. 466 p.

A survey of the relations between Church & State in Ireland
since 1922. The author examines how much influence the Roman Catholic Hierarchy has had on government policy .
See especially : " The Mother & Child Scheme ".
The author suggests that the Hierarchy has been more influ-
ential at some periods than at others, and in particular
between the late 1940s and early 1950s, when Irish Government plans in the field of public health met with forceful
opposition from the Roman Catholic Church.
Bibliography, references and Index.
Essential reading, the standard work on the subject.

WILSON, Thomas (ed.) : <u>Ulster under Home Rule : a study of the political & economic problem of Northern Ireland</u> .
1955. London. Oxford University Press. 229 p.

Essential reading.
Notes & Index. See in Appendix : Standards of public expenditure in Northern Ireland.

See also the RELEVANT CHAPTERS SECTION.

WINCHESTER, Simon : <u>In holy terror.</u>
1974. London. Faber & Faber . 256 p.

A personal account of the life of a journalist in Ulster
from April 1970 to September 1972. The author reported
daily for the <u>Manchester Guardian</u> and in 1971 was chosen
British Journalist of the Year. The period covered in this
work is one of the most formative of the present crisis
and includes " Bloody Sunday ". On that day, January 30,
1972 , 13 civilians were killed by the British Army in
Londonderry during a civil rights march (See also <u>Widgery
Report</u>. page 9 in the Official Publications Section).
Valuable information but no notes and no index.

YOUNGER, Carlton : <u>Ireland's civil war.</u>
1968. London. F.Muller. 540 p.
1970. London. Fontana (second edition).

Valuable reminiscences and information. The author makes ext-
ensive use of the British Cabinet Papers on the Irish Civil
War of 1922 - 1923 following the Anglo-Irish Treaty of 1921.
The Civil War and the Partition of Ireland which is asso-

ciated with it are two of the most controversial subjects in
Ireland even today.
Bibliography & Index.

YOUNGER, Carlton : <u>A State of Disunion</u>.
    1972. London. F.Muller. 349 p.
    1972. London. Fontana (second edition)

    Studies of four Irish political leaders :
    - Arthur Griffith (1871 - 1923)
    - Michael Collins (1890 - 1922)
    - James Craig (Lord Craigavon) 1871 - 1940
    - Eamon De Valera (1882 -)

    The actions of these four men led to much of the present
    situation in Ulster.
    Bibliography, notes, references and index.
    Valuable introduction to the subject.

    See also : DAVIS, Richard : <u>Arthur Griffith & non-violent
               Sinn Fein</u> . (page 16 in the General Works Sec-
               tion).
               FORESTER, Margery : <u>Michael Collins.The Lost
               Leader.</u> (page 30 in this section).
               ERVINE, St John : <u>Craigavon Ulsterman.</u>(page
               29 in this section).
               LONGFORD & O'NEILL : <u>Eamon De Valera.</u>(page
               37 in this section).

AKENSON, Donald Harman : <u>Once again an Ulster Question</u>.
pp. 207 - 248 in <u>The United States & Ireland</u>.
1973. Cambridge. (Mass.) Harvard University Press. 311 p.

ATKINSON, Norman : <u>Devolution in the North</u>.
pp. 177 - 193 in <u>Irish Education</u>.
1969. Dublin. A.Figgis. 246 p.

See also AKENSON,D. H : <u>Education & Enmity</u>. (page 19 in Selected Works Section)

BECKETT, J. C : <u>Northern Ireland</u>.
pp. 11 - 24 in <u>The Ulster Debate</u>. (edited by Brian Crozier & Robert Moss).
1972.London. Bodley Head. 160 p.

A concise but valuable history of Northern Ireland. A version of this paper first appeared in <u>The Journal of Contemporary History</u>.Vol.VI. No 1. pp .121 - 134 .

See also BECKETT,J. C : <u>The making of modern Ireland</u>.(page 16 in Selected Works Section)

BECKETT, J . C : <u>Carson - Unionist & Rebel</u> .
pp. 81 - 97. in <u>Leaders & Men of the Easter Rising : Dublin 1916</u>.
1967. London.Methuen. 276 p (edited by F.X.Martin)

See also : HYDE, M : <u>Life of Lord Carson</u>.(page 34)
MARJORIBANKS & COLVIN : <u>Life of Lord Carson</u> (page 40 in the Selected Works Section).

BENNETT, Jack : <u>Introduction</u>.
pp. 1 - 70 in <u>Freedom the Wolfe Tone Way</u>.
1973. Tralee. Anvil Books. 242 p.

The author, a member of the Wolfe Tone Society founded in 1963, thinks that the writings of the Protestant lawyer Wolfe Tone (1763 - 1798) are of value for analysing the present conflict. His essay " is to argue that unless Irish unity & independence are achieved, there is little hope for the future of democracy in Ireland..." Jack Bennett says that Wolfe Tone's formula for a republic is still valid. The author refutes in this passage the " two nations " theory of the British & Irish Communist Party.

BERRESFORD-ELLIS, P : <u>The Northern Revolution</u>.
pp. 308 - 326 in <u>A history of the Irish working class</u>.
1972. London. V.Gollancz. 352 p.

A socialist study of Irish history. This chapter considers the latest troubles in Northern Ireland.
Short bibliography.

BLACK, R. D. C : <u>William James Pirrie</u>.
pp. 174 - 184 in <u>The Shaping of modern Ireland</u> (edited by
C. C. O'Brien).
1960 & 1970. London .Routledge & Kegan Paul. 201 p.

The story of a successful business who helped to create the
large shipbuilding industry of Harland & Wolff in Belfast
where the Titanic was built in 1911.

BLANSHARD, Paul : <u>Northern Ireland & Partition</u>.
pp. 203 - 245 in <u>The Irish & Catholic Power</u>.
1953. Boston. The Beacon Press. 375 p.
1954. London. Dereck Verschoyle. 368 p.

A useful chapter in this standard work.

BLAXLAND, Gregory : <u>The Lone Sentry (1966 - 1970)</u>.
pp. 465 - 483 in <u>The Regiments depart</u>.
1971. London. William Kimber.

CATHERWOOD, Sir Frederick : <u>A possible settlement of the Northern Irel-
and Problem</u>.
pp. 102 - 109 in <u>The Ulster Debate</u> (edited by Brian Crozier
& Robert Moss) .
1972. London / Toronto. Bodley Head. 160 p.

The author is a former Director-General of the British National Economic Development Council (1966 - 1971) and was born
in Northern Ireland.

See also : CATHERWOOD, Sir Frederick : <u>Christian duty in Ulster today.</u> (in Pamphlets Section).

GIBSON, Norman (editor) : <u>Economic & Social implications of the political alternatives that may be
open to Northern Ireland.</u> (in Pamphlets section)

GIBSON, Norman : <u>Political possibilities for the
people of Northern Ireland.</u>(in Articles Section).

CHALFONT, Lord : <u>The balance of military forces</u>.
pp. 48 - 67 in <u>The Ulster Debate</u> (for references see above)

The author, a former Minister of State at the British Foreign & Commonwealth Office, is now military correspondent of
<u>The Times</u> newspaper.
Valuable information for the period concerned.

CLUTTERBUCK, Richard : <u>Northern Ireland - A violent contrast</u> .
pp. 47 - 123 in <u>Protest & the Urban Guerilla</u> .
1973. London. Cassell. 277 p.

The author,a retired British Major-General who served in Northern Ireland during the present crisis, is now Lecturer in
International Politics, Political Violence & Revolution at
the University of Exeter in Great-Britain.

This chapter deals with the events in the Province since 1963 to April 1972 after the introduction of Direct Rule. Brief but useful introductory notes on the different Protestant Organizations, the political parties and the Northern Ireland Civil Rights Association.
There is an analysis of urban guerilla warfare from page 104 to 109.
The work is indexed and has notes and references but no bibliography.

CONNERY, Donald : The neurotic North .
pp. 208 - 241 in The Irish.
1968. London. Eyre & Spottiswoode. 256 p.

An interesting personal account of the Province after four years under the Premiership of Capt.Terence O'Neill.

See also : O'NEILL, Terence : Ulster at the Crossroads.
and The autobiography of Terence O'Neill.
(page 42 in Selected Works Section).

COOGAN, Tim . P : The IRA (pp. 255 - 283)
The North(pp. 284 - 328) in Ireland since the Rising
1966. London. Pall Mall Press. 355 p.

The author is Editor of the Dublin daily newspaper The Irish Press.
The chapter on the IRA is a short but useful introductory essay on the subject.It covers the main three periods of activity of the Irish Republican Army , up to the end of the Border Campaign in 1962.

The chapter on Northern Ireland deals with a concise history of the state and a survey of the different political parties. It ends with an analysis of the new policy of Terence O'Neill (see above).

CRAWFORD, W. H : The rise of the linen industry.
pp. 23 - 35 in The Formation of the Irish Economy.(edited by L. M. Cullen).
1969. Cork. Mercier Press. 127 p.

Valuable short introduction to the subject. The author analyses the rise of the linen industry in the north of Ireland in the eighteenth and nineteenth centuries and its effect on the subsequent history of Ireland.
Short bibliography.

DUDLEY EDWARDS, Owen : Ireland.
pp. 5 - 209 in Celtic Nationalism.(Essays by O.Dudley Edwards; G.Evans & J.Rhys and H. MacDiarmid).
1968. London. Routledge & Kegan Paul. 358 p.

Valuable essay and historical survey of all the aspects of Irish nationalism.

FALLS, Cyril : <u>Northern Ireland and the Defence of the British Isles.</u>
pp. 79 - 114 in <u>Ulster under Home Rule</u> (edited by T.Wilson)
1955. London. Oxford University Press. 229 p.

The author,a former Professor of the History of War at Oxford,
discusses the problem raised by the fact that the Northern
Ireland Government is excluded from initiative or responsibility in the matter of defence, either in preparation or
in action.

FITZGERALD, Garret : <u>Ireland in the context of the European Community.</u>
pp. 68 - 83 in <u>The Ulster Debate</u> (edited by Brian Crozier
and Robert Moss).
1972. London / Toronto. Bodley Head. 160 p.

See also FITZGERALD, Garret : <u>Towards a new Ireland.</u>(page 29
in Selected Works Section).

FREEMAN, T. W : <u>Aspects of social geography</u> (pp. 146 - 173)
<u>Northern Ireland</u> (pp. 467 - 498)
1972. London. Methuen .559 p / 1972.New-York. Harper & Row.
in <u>Ireland : A general & regional geography.</u>

Two important chapters in this standard work. Extensive bibliography.

GAGEBY, Douglas : <u>Northern Ireland.</u>
pp. 179 - 188 in <u>Conor Cruise O'Brien introduces Ireland</u>
(edited by Owen Dudley Edwards)
1969. London. A.Deutsch. 240 p.

The author, a former editor of the Dublin daily <u>the Irish
Times</u>, is a Protestant from Belfast. He described with fo-
ndness and accuracy the land & the people.

GOLDSTROM,J. M : <u>The industrialisation of the North-East.</u>
pp. 101 - 112 in <u>The Formation of the Irish Economy.</u>
(edited by L. M . Cullen).
1969. Cork. Mercier Press. 127 p.

The author deals entirely with the nineteenth century period.

GRAY, Tony : <u>Not an inch (the Border Question).</u>
pp. 371 - 390 in <u>Ireland's Answer.</u>
1966. London. Heinemann. 411 p.

A journalist's view of the North before the latest crisis.

GREAVES, Desmond : <u>Epilogue.</u>
pp. 437 - 484 in <u>Ireland Her Own : An outline history of
the Irish struggle for national freedom & Independence.</u>
by T. A . JACKSON
1971. London. Lawrence & Wishart. 513 p.
(1946. London. Cobbett Press. First edition .)

In this epilogue the author deals especially with Ulster and
covers the period from the Partition to 1970. The work of
T. A . JACKSON ends just after the Second World War.

See also GREAVES, Desmond : <u>The Irish Crisis</u> (page 17 in
        General Works Section).

GREIG, Ian : <u>Ireland - Shape of the future</u> ?
        pp. 119 - 150 in <u>Subversion : Propaganda, agitation & the</u>
        <u>spread of the people's war.</u>
        1973. London. Tom Stacey. 202 p.

        A brief introduction to the main groups involved in the pre-
        sent crisis in Northern Ireland. Short analysis of their tac-
        tics.

HAMILTON, Cecily : <u>The Six Counties & Some of their Problems : The Oran-</u>
        <u>ge Lily and the Easter Lily.</u> (pp. 174 - 192)

                Concerning the " <u>Black North</u> " (pp. 193 - 204).
        1936. London. Dent. 239 p. <u>Modern Ireland</u>

        The first chapter (the title refers to the flowers cheris-
        hed by the Orangemen and the Republicans) surveys the foun-
        dation of Northern Ireland and the two cultures it compri-
        ses.
        The second chapter is a brief introduction to the institu-
        tions of Northern Ireland.

HAMMOND, David : <u>Industrial revolution</u> (pp. 53 - 77)
                " <u>Ulster will fight</u> " (pp. 95 - 104)
        in <u>Two centuries of Irish history.</u> (edited by J.Hawthorne)
        1966. London. BBC Publications. 136 p.

        Two programmes broadcast by the BBC for secondary schools in
        Northern Ireland.
        Notes & References and Index.

HAYWARD, Richard : <u>The Province of Ulster.</u>
        pp. 115 - 131 in   <u>Ireland by the Irish.</u> (Edited by Mauri-
        ce Gorman).
        1963. London. Galley Press. 162 p.

        A brief survey of the 9 counties of the historical province
        of Ulster.

HENRY, R. M : <u>Ulster and nationalist Ireland.</u>
        pp. 128 - 157 in <u>The Evolution of Sinn Fein.</u>
        1920. Dublin. Talbot Press. 284 p.

        The author, a former Professor of Latin at the Queen's Univer-
        sity of Belfast, analyses Irish nationalism since the death
        of Parnell.

HUTTON, J. Bernard : <u>Terror in Northern Ireland.</u>
        in   <u>The Subverters of Liberty.</u>
        1972. London. Allen.

ISLES, K. S & CUTHBERT, N : <u>Ulster's economic structure.</u>
        pp. 91 - 114 in <u>Ulster under Home Rule.</u> (edited by T.Wilson)
        1955. London. Oxford University Press. 229 p.

52

Valuable information and statistics.
See also next entry.

ISLES, K. S & CUTHBERT, N : Economic policy.
pp. 137 - 182 in Ulster under Home Rule (edited by T.Wilson)
1955. London. Oxford University Press. 229 p.

Essential reading.

KENNEDY, David : Catholics in Northern Ireland : 1926 - 1939.
pp. 138 - 149 in The Years of the Great Test :
1926 - 1939 (edited by F. MacManus).
1967. Cork. Mercier Press. 183 p.

Essential reading to understand the position and feelings of
the minority in Northern Ireland in the period concerned.

KENNEDY, David : Ulster during the war and after.
pp. 52 - 66 in Ireland in the war years and after :
1939 - 1951 . (edited by K. B. Nowlan & T. D . Williams).

See also : BLAKE, J.W : Northern Ireland in the Second World
War. (page 20 in Selected Works Section).

CARROLL, H. T : Ireland in the war years.1939 -
1945.(page 24 in Selected Works Section).

KENNEDY, David : Aspects of the northern situation.
in Irish Anglicanism. 1869 - 1969. (edited by M. Hurley)
1970. Dublin. A.Figgis.

LEES, John D. & KIMBER, Richard : Constitutions & Rules of the Ulster
Unionist Council.
in Political parties in Modern Britain (by J. D. Lees &
R. Kimber).
1972. London. Routledge & Paul .

Essential reading for detailed research.
See also : HARBINSON, John : The Ulster Unionist Party.
(page 31 in Selected Works Section).

LYONS, F. S. L : The minority problem in the 26 counties.
pp. 92 - 103 in The Years of the Great Test. 1926 -
1939. (edited by F. MacManus)
1967. Cork. Mercier Press. 183 p.

A useful chapter dealing with what the author calls " unionist in politics and mainly Protestant in religion, who
found themselves in 1921 faced with an effort of readjust-
ment far more drastic than they could have imagined five,
or even three, years earlier ".

LYONS, F. S. L : The alternatives open to Governments.
pp. 25 - 47 in The Ulster Debate (edited by Brian Crozier
and Robert Moss).
1972. London / Toronto. Bodley Head. 160 p.

See also CATHERWOOD, Sir Frederic : <u>A possible settlement of
The Northern Ireland Problem.</u> (page 49 in this
section)

Titles listed in the above entry page 49.

McCLELLAND, Aiken : <u>The later Orange Order.</u>
pp. 126 - 137 in <u>Secret Societies in Ireland</u> (edited by
T. D. Williams)
1973. Dublin. Gill & Macmillan . 207 p. / New - York. Barnes
& Noble.

The author is the Secretary of the Orange Lodge of Research.
In this chapter he deals with the period from 1860 to 1969.

See also SENIOR, Hereward : <u>Orangeism in Ireland & Britain.
1795 - 1836.</u> (page 18 in General Works Section)

GRAY, Tony : <u>The Orange Order.</u> (page 31 in Selected Works Section).

McCRACKEN, J. L : <u>Northern Ireland. 1921 - 1966.</u>
pp. 313 - 323 in <u>The Course of Irish History</u> (edited by
T. W. Moody & F. X. Martin).
1967. Cork. Mercier Press. 404 p.

A useful introductory chapter in this collection of essays
on Irish history first broadcast by the television service
of Radio Telefis Eireann in 1966.
Chronology, notes, references , bibliography and index.

McCRACKEN, J. L : <u>The political scene in Northern Ireland.1926 -1937.</u>
pp. 150 - 160 in <u>The Years of the great test.1926 - 1939.</u>
1967. Cork. Mercier Press. 183 p.

A valuable survey of the period. Essential reading.

See also : KENNEDY, David : <u>Catholics in Northern Ireland:
1926 - 1939.</u> (page 53 in this section).

McDOWELL, R. B : <u>Edward Carson.</u>
pp. 85 - 97 in <u>The Shaping of Modern Ireland</u> (edited by
Conor Cruise O'Brien).
1960 / 1970. London. Routledge & Kegan. 201 p.

See also : BECKETT,J. C : <u>Carson: Unionist & Rebel.</u> (page
48 in this section).

HYDE, M : <u>Life of Lord Carson</u> (page 34).

MARJORIBANKS & COLVIN : <u>Life of Lord Carson.</u>
(page 40 in the Selected Works Section).

MANSERGH, Nicolas : <u>The Ulster Question. 1886 - 1921.Three critical
years.</u>
pp. 182 - 217 in <u>The Irish Question. 1840 - 1921.</u>
1965. London. Allen & Unwin. 316 p.

See also : MANSERGH, Nicolas : <u>The Government of Ireland</u>

Act 1920 : its origins & purposes. (in Articles
Section).

MARTIN, F. X : McCullough, Hobson, and Republican Ulster.
   pp. 95 - 108 in Leaders & men of the Easter Rising :Dublin
   1916 (edited by F.X. Martin).
   1967. London. Methuen. 276 p.

   Valuable for the period preceding the Easter Rising , it shows
   what political attitudes were taken in the North of Ireland
   by Roman Catholics and Protestants.

MOGEY,J . M : Ulster's 6 Counties.
   pp. 1 - 13 in Ulster under Home Rule (edited by T.Wilson)
   1955. London. Oxford University Press. 229 p.

   A good but brief historical introduction in this collection
   of essays. The historical province of Ulster included 9 counties, after the Partition of Ireland, it lost Donegal,Cavan
   & Monaghan to the Irish Free State.

MOSS,Robert : Ulster : The gun speaks.
   pp. 89 - 111   in Urban guerillas : the new face of political
   violence.
   1972. London. Temple Smith. 288 p.

   An analysis of terrorism and urban guerilla warfare in the
   present crisis.

MOSS, Robert : The Ulster Debate.
   pp. 84 - 101   in   Ulster Debate (edited by Brian Crozier
   and Robert Moss).
   1972. London / Toronto. Bodley Head. 160 p.

   A valuable survey of the situation in 1971-72.

MOWATT,C. L : The Irish Question in British politics (1916 - 1922).
   pp. 141 - 152 in   The Irish Struggle . 1916 - 1926 .
   1966. London. Routledge & Kegan. 193 p.

   See also : BOYCE, D. G : Englishmen & Irish troubles:British
              Opinion & the making of the Irish policy.1918 -
              1922. (page 22 in Selected Works Section).

MURPHY, John A. : The new IRA. 1925 - 1962.
   pp. 150 - 165   in   The Secret Societies in Ireland (edited
   by T. D. Williams.
   1973. Dublin. Gill & Macmillan .217 p. / New - York. Barnes
   & Nobles.

   The author deals with the period from 1925, when the IRA assumed its independent status,to the campaign in Northern Ireland ending on February 26, 1962.

   See also : BOWYER BELL, J : The Secret Army. (page 22)

              COOGAN, Tim : The IRA. (page 25 in Selected Works
              Section).

NEWARK, F. H : <u>The law and the constitution.</u>
　　　　pp. 14 - 54 in <u>Ulster under Home Rule</u> (edited by T.Wilson).
　　　　1955. London. Oxford University Press. 229 p.

　　　　The author discusses the constitution of Northern Ireland as
　　　　a prototype of constitutional devolution which might be ap-
　　　　plied to other parts of the United Kingdom.

　　　　See also : CALVERT, Harry : <u>Constitutional law in Northern</u>
　　　　　　　　<u>Ireland.</u> (page 24 in Selected Works Section).

　　　　　　　　PALLEY, Claire : <u>The evolution, disintegration</u>
　　　　　　　　<u>And possible reconstruction of the Northern</u>
　　　　　　　　<u>Ireland constitution.</u>(in Pamphlets Section)

　　　　　　　　QUECKETT, Sir Arthur : <u>The Constitution of</u>
　　　　　　　　<u>Northern Ireland.</u> (page 3 in Bibliographies
　　　　　　　　& Reference Works Section).

NORMAN, Edward : <u>The divided nation.</u>
　　　　pp. 289 - 314 in <u>A history of modern Ireland.</u>
　　　　1971. London. Allen Lane. 330 p.
　　　　1973. Harmondsworth. Pelican Books. 330 p.

　　　　A controversial view of Irish history.
　　　　Short bibliography.

O'BRIEN ,Leon : <u>The Ulster Question. 1913 - 1914.</u>
　　　　pp. 81 - 113 in <u>The Chief Secretary : Augustine Birrell</u>
　　　　<u>in Ireland.</u>
　　　　1969. London. Chatto & Windus. 232 p. / Toronto. Clarke,Irwin
　　　　& Co.

　　　　Augustine Birrell was Chief Secretary of Ireland from 1907
　　　　to 1916, when the Easter Rising took place in Dublin.

PAKENHAM, Frank (Lord Longford) : <u>The treaty negotiations.</u>
　　　　pp. 107 - 115 in <u>The Irish Struggle.1916 - 1926</u> (edited
　　　　by T. D. Williams).
　　　　1966. London. Routledge & Kegan. 193 p.

　　　　See also LONGFORD, Lord : <u>Peace by Ordeal : The negotiations</u>
　　　　　　　　<u>of the Anglo - Irish Treaty 1921.</u> (page 36, in
　　　　　　　　Selected Works Section).

SAYERS, J. E : <u>The political parties and the social background.</u>
　　　　pp. 55 - 78 in <u>Ulster under Home Rule</u> (edited by T.Wilson)
　　　　1955. London. Oxford University Press. 229 p.

　　　　Essential reading. The author deals with the period from 1920
　　　　to 1954. He was for some years on the Prime Minister's perso-
　　　　nal staff under Winston Churchill and was managing editor of
　　　　<u>The Belfast Telegraph</u> when he wrote this essay.

STACK, Austin : <u>Journal of the Big Belfast Jail Riot.</u>
　　　　pp. 76 - 82 in <u>The Complete Book of IRA Jailbreaks 1918</u>
　　　　<u>1921.</u>
　　　　1971. Tralee. Anvil Books. 207 p.

The author, a staunch republican, while in Belfast Jail, in
1918, was elected TD for West Kerry and was subsequently the
Minister for Home Affairs who set up the Dail Courts. He died
in 1929.
Austin Stack tells the story of the riots which took place
in Belfast main prison, Crumlin Road Jail, between May 1918
and April 1919.

STEWART, A. T. Q : Craig and the Ulster Volunteer Force.
    pp. 67 - 80 in Leaders & Men of the Easter Rising : Dublin
    1916. (edited by F.X. Martin).
    1967. London. Methuen. 276 p.

   See also : STEWART, A. T. Q : The Ulster Crisis (page 44 in
       Selected Works Section).

WALL, Maureen : Partition : the Ulster Question. 1916 - 1926.
    pp. 79 - 93 in The Irish Struggle. 1916 - 1926.(edited
    by T. D. Williams).
    1966. London. Routledge & Kegan. 193 p.

   See also : North Eastern Boundary Bureau : Handbook of the
       Ulster Question. (page 3 in Bibliographies and
       Reference Works Section).

       Report of the Irish Boundary Commission.1925.
       (page 3)

       GALLAGHER, Frank : The Indivisible Island.
       (page 30 in Selected Works Section).

       JONES, Thomas : Whitehall Diary.Vol.3 (page 34
       in Selected Works Section)

WALLACE, Martin : Northern Ireland.
    pp. 122 - 130 in Two Centuries of Irish History. (edited
    by J. Hawthorne).
    1966. London. BBC Publications. 136 p.

  This lecture was first broadcast on BBC radio in Northern
  Ireland as a programme for secondary schools.

   See also : WALLACE, Martin : Northern Ireland : 50 years of
       self - government. (page 45 in Selected Works
       Section).

WALSH, Brendan. M : Migration between Northern Ireland and the Republic
    of Ireland.
    in Religion & Demographic behaviour in Ireland.
    1970. Dublin. Economic & Social Research Institute.

  Essential reading for detailed research.

WILLIAMS, T. Desmond : The Irish Republican Brotherhood .
    pp. 138 - 149 in Secret Societies in Ireland (edited by
    T.D Williams.)
    1973. Dublin. Dublin. Gill & Macmillan. 217 p. / New - York.
    Barnes & Nobles.

The author surveys the period from 1858 to 1924. This secret
organization took a prominent part in the Dublin Easter Rising
in 1916.

WILSON, Thomas : Devolution & Public Finance.(pp. 115 - 136)
                 Devolution & Partition . (pp. 183 - 211)
    in Ulster under Home Rule (edited by T. Wilson)
    1955. London. Oxford University Press. 229 p.

    Essential reading.

7 - <u>ARTICLES</u>

<u>ANARCHY</u> : Special issue on Ireland.
1971. London. Vol.i. No 6. Second series. 36p.

ANDREWS, J. H : <u>The ' Morning Post ' Line</u>.
pp. 99 - 106
in <u>Irish Geography</u>. 1960. Dublin.

ANDREWS, J. H : <u>The papers of the Irish Boundary Commission</u>.
pp. 477 - 481
in <u>Irish Geography</u>. 1968. Dublin

See also : <u>Report of the Irish Boundary Commission</u>.
(page 3 in Bibliographies & Reference Works Section).

ARMSTRONG, D. L : <u>Social & Economic conditions in the Belfast linen industry</u>.
in <u>Irish Historical Studies</u>. Sept. 1951. Vol.vii. No 28.

See also : CRAWFORD, W. H: <u>The rise of the linen industry</u>.
(page 50 in Relevant Chapters).

ARNOLD, Bruce : <u>The Two Irelands : A special report</u>.
pp. 419 - 421
in <u>Britannica Book of the Year 1971</u>. London.

A summary of the events of 1970.

BALL, David : <u>Warfare welfare</u>.
in <u>New Society</u>. 16 dec. 1971. London.

The difficulties of normal life and normal social work during the troubles.

BARRINGTON, Donal : <u>Council of Ireland in the Constitutional context</u>.
pp. 28 - 49
in <u>Administration</u>. Dublin. Winter 1972. vol. xx. No 4

The author, a lawyer, examines the Council of Ireland as envisaged in the Government of Ireland Act 1920 and how it could be implemented in the context of the EEC and what its functions would be.

See also : <u>The Sunningdale Agreement</u>.(page 11 in Official Publications Section).

MANSERGH, Nicolas : <u>The Government of Ireland Act 1920 : its origins & purposes. The working of the ' official ' mind</u>. (See this section).

BARRITT, Denis : <u>1961 - 1971 : Progress or retrogression</u> ?
pp. 14 - 18 .
in <u>Community Forum</u>.Belfast. Northern Ireland Community Relations Commission. Vol i. No 2. 1971.

The author,with C.F. Carter, has written one of the best study of Protestant - Catholics relations in Northern Ireland. See The Northern Ireland Problem (page 19 in Selected Works Section).
Denis Barritt considers how the problem has altered since the book was published.

BAILEY, John & LOIZOS, Peter : Bogside off its knees. in New Society . London. 21 Aug. 1969.

Sociological observation on the street fighting in August 1969 in the Roman Catholic district of Londonderry.

See also : LIMPKIN, C : The Battle of the Bogside.

STETLER, R : The Battle of the Bogside.
(page 36 & 44 in Selected Works Section)

BENN, John : The commissioner for complaints. pp. 20 - 21 in Community Forum. Belfast. NICRC. vol. ii No 1. 1972.

BOWYER, Bell, J : The Chroniclers of violence : the troubles in Northern Ireland interpreted. pp. 28 - 38 in EIRE - IRELAND . St Paul (Minnesota). Vol.vii. No 1 . Spring 1972.

The author of The Secret Army (See page 22 in Selected Works Section) analyses the boom in the publishing industry on the troubles in Northern Ireland .

BIRRELL, W. D & MURIE, A : Social services in Northern Ireland . pp. 107 - 132 in Administration. Dublin. Winter 1972. Vol. xx . No 4

Valuable statistics . Northern Ireland has since 1945 participated in what has become known as the British " Welfare State ".

BIRRELL, W. D & Others : The Northern Ireland Housing Executive. pp. 274 - 284 in Administration. Dublin. 1971. Vol xix. No 3.

Essential reading for introduction to the subject.

BIRRELL, W. D & Others : Housing in Northern Ireland. University Working Paper 12. 1971. London. Centre for Environmental Studies.

Essential reading for detailed research.

BLAKSTAD, Michael : Children in crossfire. pp. 321 - 324 in The Listener. London. 14 march 1974. Vol.91. No 2346

This article is based on a BBC Television documentary

investigating the lives of 30,000 children living in Northern
Ireland's most troubled areas.

BLEAKLEY, David : The Northern Ireland Trade Union Movement.
in Journal of the Statistical & Social Inquiry Society of
Ireland.
Vol. xx. 1959 - 1960.

See also : BOYD, A : The rise of the Irish trade unions.
(page 22 in Selected Works Section).

BOAL, F. W : Territoriality on the Shankill-Falls Divide, Belfast.
pp. 30 - 50
in Irish Geography. Dublin. 1969. Vol. vi. No 1.

Essential reading for detailed research. The author examines
two famous districts of Belfast. Both are working-class areas
well-known for their feelings : The Shankill Road is the
main thoroughfare of a Protestant area and the Falls is its
equivalent on the Roman Catholic side of this area of West
Belfast. Both streets run along a " Peace - Line " which was
built in 1969 by the British Army. This wall is made of cor-
rugated iron, barbed wire and concrete. It is a mile and a
half long.

BOAL, F. W : Territoriality & class : a study of two residential areas
in Belfast.
pp. 229 - 248
in Irish Geography. Dublin. 1971. Vol. vi. No 3

Complementary to the article mentioned above.

BOAL, F. W : Social space in the Belfast urban area.
in Irish Geographical Studies. 1970. Dept of Geography.
Queen's University . Belfast.

BOAL, F. W & BUCHANAN, R. H : Conflict in Northern Ireland.
pp. 331 - 336
in Geographical Magazine. London. February 1969.

BOAL, F. W & BUCHANAN, R. H : The 1969 Northern Ireland Election.
pp. 78 - 84
in Irish Geography. Dublin. 1969. Vol vi. No 1

The 1969 election for the Stormont Parliament was a turning
point in the civil rights campaign and the present crisis.
Some of the Roman Catholic leaders who have emerged since,
such as Patrick Devlin and John Hume, were elected then. At
the same time the Protestant leader, the Reverend Ian Paisley was polling 1,414 less against the Prime Minister, Terence O'Neill.
Essential reading.

BOEHRINGER, Gill : The future of policing in Northern Ireland.
pp. 20 - 24
in Community Forum. Belfast. NICRC. 1973. Vol iii. No 2.

Since 1969, following the riots and the reform of the police, policing has been the subject of much controversy despite the innovations introduced by the Hunt Report (See page 6, in Official Publications Section).

BOSERUP, A & IVERSEN, C : Rank analysis of a polarised community : A case study from Northern Ireland.
pp. 59 - 76
in International Papers.Peace Research Society. Vol.vii

BOWEN, Desmond : The Ballymurphy Estate.
pp. 270 - 272
in Contemporary Review.London. May 1971. Vol.218. No 1264.

One of the most troubled areas of Belfast, the Ballymurphy estate was built in the early 1950's and housed mostly Roman Catholics. Since the beginning of the troubles it has been the scene of numerous riots and the 'mixed' areas of the estate (ie.where Protestants and Roman Catholics were living) soon turned into a Roman Catholic ghetto. During the unrest the whole estate was ruled by the " Provisionals " of the IRA and patrolled by the British Army. Today very few Protestants live there.

See also : SPENCER, A.E.C : Ballymurphy. (in Pamphlets section).

BOYCE, D. G : British Conservative Opinion, the Ulster Question & the Partition of Ireland. 1912 - 1921.
pp. 89 - 112
in Irish Historical Studies. Dublin. March 1970. Vol 17. No 65.

See also : BOYCE, D. G : English Men & Irish Troubles.
(page 22 in Selected Works Section).

BOYD, Andrew : The guilty men of Ulster.
in Everyman.Dungannon. 1970. No 3.

A strong attack against Ulster Unionists.

BOYD, Andrew : Time to end Stormont.
p.4
in Irish Weekly. Belfast. February 7, 1970.

BOYD, Andrew : The Orangeman & his enemies.
pp. 97 - 99
in Aquarius. Benburb. 1971. No 4 .

The author of Holy War in Belfast (see page 22 in Selected Works Section) takes a hard look at the venerable Northern institution.

BOYD, Andrew : <u>Belfast riots 1935</u>.
        pp. 107 - 109
        in <u>Aquarius</u>. Benburb. 1972. No 5

        Useful background information on the period concerned.

        See also : <u>For Members of Parliament</u>. (page 19 in Selected
        Works Section).
                ULTACH : <u>The Persecution of Catholics in Northern
                Ireland</u>. (in this section).
                ULTACH : <u>Orange Terror</u>. (in Pamphlets Section).

BOYLE, J : <u>The Belfast Protestant association and the Independent Oran-
        ge Order</u>.
        in <u>Irish Historical Studies</u>. Dublin. Sept. 1962. vol.xiii.

        See also : SENIOR, H : <u>Orangeism in Ireland & in Britain</u>.

                GRAY, T : <u>The Orange Order</u>.

                DEWAR, BROWN & LONG : <u>Orangeism : a new histori-
                cal appreciation</u>.

                (In Selected Works Section : p.18; p.31; p.27)

BOYLE, Kevin : <u>Northern Ireland : dismantling the Protestant state</u>.
        pp. 12 - 18
        in <u>New Blackfriars</u>. London. Jan.1971. No 52.

        The author was a prominent member of the People's Democracy
        movement, he is now a barrister and a lecturer at Queen's
        University,Belfast.

        See also : ARTHUR, P : <u>The People's Democracy</u>. (page 19 in
                Selected Works Section).

BRADFORD, Roy : <u>Foundations for progress</u>.
        pp. 61 - 63
        in <u>Administration</u>. Dublin. Winter 1972. vol. xx. No 4

        A former Minister of State in the Stormont Cabinet (from
        24. 1. 1969 to 24. 3. 1972) the author believes that Euro-
        pe will help to find a solution to the Northern Ireland pro-
        blem.

        See also : FITZGERALD, G : <u>Ireland in the context of the Euro-
                pean Community</u>. (page 51 in Relevant Chapters Sec-
                tion).

BRETT, C. E. : <u>The lessons of devolution in Northern Ireland</u>.
        in <u>Political Quaterly</u>. London. July-Sept. 1970. Vol.41. No 3

        See also : WILSON, T : <u>Ulster under home rule</u>.
                LAWRENCE, R. J : <u>The Government of Northern Ireland;
                Public finance & Public services</u>.
                (in Selected Works Section : p.46 ; p.36)

BUCHANAN, R. H : <u>Five year plan for Ulster</u>.
    pp. 845 - 6
    in <u>Geographical Magazine</u> . London. Aug.1970.

    An analysis of the Development Programme for Northern Ireland
    1970 - 1975 (see page 8 in Official Publications Section).

BUSTEED, M. A : <u>Re-shaping Belfast's local government</u>.
    in <u>Administration</u>. Dublin. 1970. vol 18. No 3

    See also the <u>Macrory Report</u> (page 8 in Official Publications
    Section).

BUSTEED, M. A & MASON, Hugh : <u>Local government reform in Northern Ire-
    land</u> .
    in <u>Irish Geography</u>.Dublin. 1971. vol.vi. No 3

    See also entry mentioned above.

CAHILL, Gilbert A : <u>Some 19th century roots of the Ulster problem</u>.
    <u>1829 - 1848</u>.
    pp. 215 - 237
    in <u>Irish University Review</u>. Dublin. 1971. Vol.1.

    Essential reading for detailed research. This article would
    serve as a good introduction to the subject.

CALVERT, Harry : <u>What Sunningdale means in terms of law</u>.
    in the <u>Belfast Telegraph.</u> February 5-9, 1974.

    See also the <u>Sunningdale Agreement</u> (page 11 in Official
              Publications Section).

CARTER, Charles F : <u>Permutations of Government</u>.
    pp.50 - 57
    in <u>Administration</u>. Dublin. Winter 1972. Vol xx. No 4

    The author proposes the idea of a condominium for Northern
    Ireland.

CATHCART, Rex : <u>To build anew</u>.
    pp. 43 - 46
    in <u>The Northern Teacher</u>. Belfast. Winter 1973.

    The role of Northern Ireland schools in helping children set-
    tle in society.

CHALFONT, Lord Alun : <u>The Army & the IRA</u>.
    pp. 147 - 148
    in <u>New Statesman</u>. London. April 2, 1971.

    An analysis by the London <u>Times</u> Military Correspondent.

COMMUNITY FORUM : <u>Special issue on " The Two Cultures in Ulster "</u>.
    pp. 9 - 28
    in <u>Community Forum</u>. Belfast. NICRC. 1974. Vol.4. No 1

From the introduction : " The question of cultural & national
identity is one which has tortured Ulster people for genera-
tions." This special issue analyses cultural identity in Northern Ireland as it has been seen by poets, novelists, artis-
ts, folk experts and educationalists.

COMMUNITY FORUM : Special issue on " West of the Bann : Derry city ".
pp. 2 - 30
in Community Forum. Belfast. NICRC. 1974. vol.4. No 2

Geographically Northern Ireland is cut in half from North to
South by the Bann River and Lough Neagh. Plantations of Scots
Presbyterian settled on the East side whereas Roman Catholics
(the natives) fled to the west side.
This issue analyses the background, institutions, activities
and people of the city of Londonderry famous for its siege
in 1689 and where rioting developed on such a scale that British troops were brought in on August 14, 1969.

COMMUNITY FORUM : Special issue on " West of the Bann : county and
small communities.
pp. 30 - 36.
in Community Forum.Belfast. NICRC. 1974. Vol.4. No 2

This section deals with community activity around the town of
Dungannon , rural development and schoolboys in the West.

COOPER, Ronald & O'SHEA, Theresa : Northern Ireland : A NEW SOCIETY
SURVEY OF the social trends.
pp. 552 - 558
in NEW SOCIETY. London. June 1973. vol.24 No 557

Two sociology lecturers analyse the underlying social trends
of Northern Ireland. Valuable statistics .

COUGHLAN, Antony : A comment on North-South comparisons.
pp. 133 - 135
in Administration. Dublin. Winter 1972. Vol.20. No 4

This survey applies only to social services.

CURRAN, Joseph M : Lloyd George and the Irish settlement 1921 - 1922.
pp. 14 - 26
in Eire-Ireland. St Paul (Minnesota). Vol 7 No 2.

See also : LLOYD, George : War memoirs.

LONGFORD, Lord : Peace by Ordeal.

JONES, T : Whitehall diary.vol.3
(See Selected Works Section : p.36 ; p.34)

DALLAT, Michael & MOLES, William : FORUM DEBATE : Integrated education.
pp. 16 - 19
in Community Forum. Belfast. NICRC. 1972. vol.2. No 1

See also : AKENSON, D : Education & Enmity. (page 19 in Selected Works Section).

CONWAY, Cardinal : <u>Catholic Schools.</u> (In Pamphlets
Section)

DARBY, John : <u>Divisiveness in education.</u>
pp. 3 - 12
in <u>The Northern Teacher.</u> Belfast. Winter 1973.

The author examines the numerous educational divides in Northern Ireland.

DAVIES, Stan Gebler : <u>Ulster '71 : Festival of faith.</u>
pp. 664 - 666
in <u>The Spectator.</u> London. May 15, 1971.

In 1971 the Northern Ireland Government organized a festival
to celebrate the 50th anniversary of the Northern Ireland state.

See also : People's Democracy : <u>The Real Ulster 1971.</u> (in
Pamphlets Section).

DE PAOR, Liam : <u>Cultural traditions.</u>
pp. 140 - 152
in <u>Administration.</u> Dublin. Winter 1972. Vol.20. No 4

The author discusses the myths surrounding the code words
" gaelic " & " British ".

See also his current series of articles <u>Roots</u> in the daily
Dublin newspaper <u>The Irish Times.</u>

DEUTSCH, Richard : <u>As others see us : France.</u>
pp. 3 - 6
in <u>Community Forum.</u> Belfast. NICRC. 1974. vol.4 No 1

A survey of the coverage by French media of the troubles in
Northern Ireland since 1968.

DIAMOND, Harry : <u>What is the future of the UDR</u> ?
p.4
in <u>Irish Weekly.</u> Belfast. January 17, 1970.

The author was a Nationalist MP at the Stormont Parliament.
The Ulster Defence Regiment (6,000 strong) was created by
the Westminster Government in November 1969 to replace the
B-Specials. Recruiting started in January 1970 and the UDR
took up its official duties on April 30, 1970 when the Special Constabulary was officially stood down.

See also : <u>The Hunt Report</u> (Page 6 in Official Publications
Section).

DICKEY, Anthony : <u>Anti-incitement legislation in Britain & Northern
Ireland.</u>
pp. 133 - 138
in <u>New Community.</u>London. January 1972. Vol.1 No 2

DONNISON, David : The Northern Ireland civil service.
    pp. 8 - 10
    in New Society. London. July 1973. vol.25. No 651

    An analysis showing that there is not enough Roman Catholics
    in the Northern Ireland Civil Service.

DUDLEY EDWARDS, Owen : A look at Reverend Ian Paisley.
    pp. 11 - 16
    in Nusight. Dublin. May 1970.

    An analysis of the political rise of the Reverend Ian Paisley
    following his election at Bannside ,Co.Antrim on April 17,1970.
    The author examines the contents of his newspaper, The Protes-
    tant Telegraph.
    A valuable article on the Reverend Ian Paisley.

    See also : MARRINAN, P: Paisley : Man of wrath. (page 40
                in Selected Works Section)

DWYER, T. Ryle : The Anglo-Irish Treaty and why they signed it.
    pp. 333 - 372
    in Capucin Annual. Dublin. vol.38

    See also : CURRAN, J : Lloyd George & the Irish settlement
                1921 - 1922. (page 65, in this section).

                (See also titles mentioned in this entry).

ECONOMIST , The : Ulster. A survey.
    in The Economist. London. May 29, 1971 . No 6666. Vol. 239

    A political & economic survey by the leading British finan-
    cial weekly.

    See also : LEE, Gordon & TAYLOR, Robert : Ulster. (in Pam-
                phlets Section).

ELCOCK, H. J : Opportunity for Ombudsman : The Northern Ireland Com-
    missioner for complaints.
    pp. 87 - 93
    in Public Administration. London. 1972. Vol.50

    Sir Edmund Compton, the first Northern Ireland Ombudsman,
    took office on July 1, 1969.

    See also : BENN, J : The Commissioner for complaints. (page
                60, in this section).

ELLIOTT, Sidney : Northern Ireland 's elections : The Assembly's
    Heritage.
    pp. 28 - 32
    in Community Forum. Belfast. NICRC. 1973. Vol.3. No 3

    An analysis of the results of the Northern Ireland Assembly
    elections held in June 1973 under Proportional Representa-
    tion. Thsi 78 seat assembly was to replace the old Stormont
    Parliament. The author concludes that despite the reintro-

duction of Proportional Representation the results showed
many similarities to the elections which had taken place
earlier in the Province.

See also : KNIGHT, J : <u>Northern Ireland : The elections of
1973</u>.(in Pamphlets Section).

EVANS, Estyn E : <u>The Northern Heritage</u>.
pp. 51 - 56
in <u>Aquarius</u>. Benburb. 1971.

A short survey of the Northern cultures by the retired Director of the Institute of Irish Studies at Queen's University
Belfast.

See also : EVANS, E.E : <u>The personality of Ireland</u>. (page 16
in General Works Section).

EVANS, Estyn E : <u>Belfast. The site and the city</u>.
pp. 25 - 29
in <u>Ulster Journal of Archaeologists</u>. Belfast. 1944. (III
series). Vol.7.

See also : GLASSCOCK,E.R & BECKETT,J.C : <u>Belfast. Origin &
Growth</u>.(page 17 in General Works Section).

EVANS, Estyn E & JONES, E : <u>The growth of Belfast</u>.
pp. 93 - 111
in <u>Town Planning Review</u>. London. 1955.

See also previous entry.

FAIR, John D : <u>The King, the Constitution and Ulster : interparty negotiations of 1913 & 1914.</u>
pp. 35 - 52
in <u>Eire-Ireland</u>. St Paul (Minnesota). Spring 1971. Vol.6 No1

George V and the Irish Question.

See also : STEWART,A.T.Q : <u>The Ulster Crisis</u>.(page 44 in Selected Works Section).

FAIR, John D : <u>The Anglo-Irish Treaty of 1921 : unionist aspects of the
peace.</u>
pp. 132 - 149
in <u>Journal of British Studies</u>. London. vol.12 (Symposium :
Ireland & British Politics. 1914 - 1921. III).

See also : DWYER,T: <u>The Anglo-Irish Treaty and why they signed it.</u>

CURRAN,J : <u>Lloyd George and the Irish settlement</u>
(In this Section : p.67 ; p.65)

FANNING, J. R : <u>The Unionist Party & Ireland. 1906 - 1910</u>.
in <u>Irish Historical Studies</u>. Dublin. Sept.1966. Vol.15

See also : HARBINSON, J : <u>The Ulster Unionist Party</u>.(page 31 in Selected Works Section).

FAULKNER, Brian : Ireland today.
  pp.86 - 90
  in Aquarius. Benburb. 1971.

  A Unionist point of view by a former Northern Ireland Prime
  Minister.

   See also : BLEAKELEY, D : Brian Faulkner.(page 21 in Selec-
    ted Works Section).

FEENEY, Vincent E : The civil rights movement in Northern Ireland.
  pp.30 - 40
  in Eire-Ireland.St Paul (Minnesota). Summer 1974. vol 9. No2

  The rise of the civil rights movement from 1966.

   See also : HEATLEY, Fred : - Civil rights in the 6 Counties.
              - The Civil rights story
    (In this section).

    HASTINGS, Max : Ulster 1969. The fight for civil
    rights in Northern Ireland.

FENNELL, Desmond : The failure of the Irish Revolution & its success.
  pp. 334 - 343

  (and also comments on this article : pp. 344 - 352)
  in The Capucin Annual. Dublin. 1964.

  A survey of the period following 1916.

FIELDS, Rona : Ulster : a psychological experiment ?
  pp. 445 - 448
  in New Humanist. London. March 1973. vol.88. No 11

  Rona Fields, an american psychologist, argues that techniques
  of social control and " unarmed combat " are used in Northern
  Ireland.

   See also : FIELDS, R : A society on the run. (page 29 in
    Selected Works Section).

FRASER, R. M : Psychiatric sequelae of the 1969 Belfast riots.
  pp.16 - 19
  in British Journal of Psychiatry. London. March 1971.
  vol. 118 No 544
  (reprinted in Community Forum. Belfast. NICRC. 1971.vol.1.No1)

  Essential reading for detailed research.

   See also : FRASER, R. M : Children in Conflict. (page 30 in
    Selected Works Section).

    LYONS,H.A : The psychological effects of the civil
    disturbances on children. (In this section).

FRASER, R. M : <u>Ulster's children of conflict.</u>
in <u>NEW SOCIETY.</u>London. April 15, 1971.

Symptoms of the children affected by the troubles.

FREEMAN, T. W : <u>The man-made walls of Ulster.</u>
pp. 594 - 599
in <u>Geographical Magazine.</u> London. Aug. 1974. Vol.46. No 11

The author examines the sectarian division of the province.

GIBBON, Peter : <u>Ireland - Split in Sinn Fein</u> .
pp. 49 - 52
in <u>New Left Review.</u>London. March - April 1970.

At the end of 1969 the Irish Republican Army split in two
organizations : The Provisional IRA & The Official IRA. Their
political counterparts, Sinn Fein, became known as Sinn Fein
Provisional (Kevin St) and Sinn Fein Official (Gardiner
St).

See also : SINN FEIN (Kevin ST) & SINN FEIN (Gardiner St)
(in Pamphlets Section).

GIBSON, Norman : <u>Constitution building in Ireland.</u>
pp. 5 - 17
in <u>Administration.</u> Dublin. Winter 1972. Vol.20. No 4

The author, Professor of Economics at the New University of
Ulster (Coleraine), envisages in this study North and
South participating in a new constitution.

GIBSON, Norman : <u>Political possibilities for the people of Northern</u>
<u>Ireland.</u>
pp. 64 - 71
in <u>Administration.</u> Dublin. Winter 1972. Vol.20. No 4

The search for a peaceful and stable solution.

See also : CATHERWOOD, F : <u>A possible settlement of the</u>
<u>Northern Ireland Problem.</u>

LYONS, F. S. L : <u>The alternatives open to</u>
<u>Governments.</u>
(In Relevant chapters Section : p.49 ; p.53)

GIBSON, N : <u>Economic and Social implications of</u>
<u>the political alternatives that may be open to</u>
<u>Northern Ireland.</u> (In Pamphlets Section).

GIBSON, Norman : <u>Note on financial relationships between Britain and</u>
<u>Northern Ireland.</u>
pp. 136 - 139
in <u>Administration.</u> Dublin. Winter 1972. Vol.20 No 4

Until the publication on September 10th, 1974 of <u>Northern</u>
<u>Ireland : Finance & the Economy</u> (See page 12 in Official
Publications Section) there was much controversy about

the figures available.

GIBSON, Norman : <u>The Northern Problem. Religious or Economic or what</u> ?
pp. 2 - 5
in <u>Community Forum</u>. Belfast. NICRC. 1971. Vol.1 No 1

This is an amended version of a talk given in November 1970.
Essential reading.

GILLMAN, Peter : <u>The Quiet Man</u> .
pp. 8 - 18
in <u>The Sunday Times Magazine</u>. London. July 30, 1972.

A rare portrait of John Lynch who was Prime Minister of the
Irish Republic from 1966 to 1973.

See also : LYNCH, J : <u>Speeches & Statements : Irish unity</u>
<u>Northern Ireland, anglo-Irish relations. August</u>
<u>1969 - October 1971</u>.
(page 13 in Official Publications Section).

GILLMAN, Peter : <u>In Belfast there are only losers</u>.
pp. 23 - 28
in <u>The Sunday Times Magazine</u>. London. August 13, 1972.

Interviews of families who have lost relatives following the
troubles.

GRACE, Edmond : <u>Responsibility and consent</u>.
pp. 153 - 160
in <u>Administration</u>. Dublin. Winter 1972. Vol.20 No 4

The author, a former President of the Irish Association, urges
people to examine in public debate the future structure of
government in Ireland.
The Irish Association was founded in 1938 to promote cultural
and economic and social relations in Ireland.

GRAY, Tony : <u>Besieged, betrayed ... and bewildered</u>.
pp. 436 - 438
in <u>New Humanist</u>. London. March 1973. Vol.88. No 11

The author argues that the Ulster Protestant has been left in
limbo historically, socially, politically and economically.

See also : GRAY, T : <u>The Orange Order</u>. (page 31 in Selected
Works Section).

SIMMS, J. G : <u>Remembering 1690</u>. (in this section)

WRIGHT, F : <u>Protestant ideology and politics in</u>
<u>Ulster</u>. (in this section).

GREAVES, Desmond : <u>Preface</u>.
in <u>Marx & Engels on Ireland</u>.
1971. Moscow. Progress Publishers. 518 p./ Lawrence & Wishart.
London.

The author explains the importance of the writings of Karl
Marx and Frederick Engels for the understanding of the pre-

sent situation in Northern Ireland.

  See also : GREAVES, D : <u>The Irish Crisis</u>. (page 17 in Gener-
    al Works Section)

          <u>Epilogue</u> (page 51 in Relevant Chap-
    ters Section).

GREER, D. S : <u>Legal aid for summary trials in Northern Ireland</u>.
    pp. 431 - 458
    in <u>Northern Ireland Legal Quaterly</u>. Belfast. Vol.22. Winter
    1971. No 4

GRIFFITHS, Hywel : <u>Community Development and Community Relations</u>.
    pp. 3 - 7
    in <u>Community Forum</u>. Belfast. NICRC. 1971. Vol. 1 No 2

    A former Director of the Northern Ireland Community Relations
    Commission explains the strategy of community development in
    Northern Ireland.

GRIFFITHS, Hywel : <u>The Northern Ireland Community Relations Commission</u>.
    pp. 128 - 132
    in <u>New Community</u>. London. Jan. 1972. Vol.1. No 2

    The Northern Ireland Community Relations Commission was set
    up by the Northern Ireland Government at the end of 1969.

    See also previous entry.

GUTHRIE, Sir Tyrone : <u>The Belfast Character</u>.
    pp. 11 - 13
    in <u>IN BRITAIN</u>.London. February 1971. Vol.26. No 2

    The author was a leading British actor, born in Belfast.

HACHEY, Thomas E : <u>The British Foreign Office & new perspectives of</u>
    <u>the Irish issue in Anglo-American relations. 1919 - 1921</u>.
    pp. 3 - 13
    in <u>Eire - Ireland</u>. St Paul (Minnesota). vol.7. No 2

    See also : CURRAN,J. M : <u>Llyod George and the Irish settle-</u>
      ment 1921 - 1922.

      DWYER, T. R : <u>The Anglo-Irish Treaty and why they</u>
      signed it.

      FAIR,J.D : <u>The Anglo-Irish Treaty of 1921</u> : unio-
      nist aspects of the peace.

      (In this section : p.65; p.67; p.68)

HADDEN, Tom : <u>Interlocking Ulstermen</u>.
    in <u>New Society</u>. London. February 17, 1972.

    The author examines why the two communities in Northern Ire-
    land always refer back to 1690 and beyond and also to reli-
    gion.
    Essential reading.

See also : SIMMS, J. G : <u>Remembering 1690.</u>

WRIGHT, F : <u>Protestant Ideology and Politics in</u>
<u>Ulster.</u>
(In this section) .

HANSON, Richard : <u>Politics & the Pulpit</u> .
pp. 14 - 18
in <u>Community Forum.</u> Belfast. NICRC. 1973. Vol.3. No 3

This article is reprinted from the daily newspaper <u>The Guar-</u>
<u>dian.</u>
The author, a member of the Church of Ireland, is Bishop of
Clogher. He analyses to what extent the Churches have contri-
buted to the Northern Ireland situation.

See also : PAISLEY, Rev. : <u>The case against ecumenisn.</u>

WILSON, Fr. : <u>The sixties: the years of oppor-</u>
<u>tunity.</u>
(In this section).

HARKIN, Brendan : <u>Political possibilities for the people of Northern</u>
<u>Ireland.</u>
pp. 79 - 85
in <u>Administration.</u> Dublin. Winter 1972. Vol.20. No 4

The author, a leading Belfast trade unionist, is one of Ireland's representatives on the EEC's Economic and Social Committee.

HARRISON, Paul : <u>Culture & Migration : the Irish English.</u>
in <u>New Society.</u> London. Sept. 1973.

The Irish are one of the main immigrant groups in Britain.
Most of them remain distinct but the author argues that the
Irish community in Birmingham shows integration's stages.
On Thursday 21st November 1974, bombs placed in bars in Birmingham killed 21 persons. It was generally thought that the
bombings had been masterminded by the Provisional IRA, although so far the movement never admitted it. Following the
bombings there was a strong anti-Irish feeling in English
cities such as Birmimgham, Liverpool and Manchester.

HAYES, Maurice : <u>The role of the community relations commission in</u>
<u>Northern Ireland.</u>
pp. 86 - 106
in <u>Administration.</u> Dublin. Winter 1972. Vol.20 No 4

The author was for some time a director of the Northern Ireland Community Relations Commission.
A useful introduction to the subject.

See also : GRIFFITHS, H : <u>The Northern Ireland Community</u>
<u>Relations Commission.</u> (page 72 in this section).

<u>Community development and Com-</u>
<u>munity Relations.</u> (page 72 in this section).

HEALY, John : Ireland - A double dilemma.
          pp. 62 - 64
          in Aquarius. Benburb. 1972.

          The author is parliamentary correspondent for the Dublin
          daily newspaper The Irish Times . Under the pen-name
          " Backbencher " he writes every week one of the best poli-
          cal columns of Ireland.

HEATLEY, Fred : Civil rights in the 6 Counties.
          pp. 77 - 80
          in The Significance of Freedom. Celtic League Annual. 1969.
          Dublin.

          The author is a former Secretary of the Northern Ireland
          Civil Rights Association.

HEATLEY, Fred : The Civil Rights Story.
          in Fortnight Magazine.Belfast. 1974. No 80 - 84.

          A series of articles on the NICRA . From the foundation of
          the organization to the present day.
          The author covers in details the foundation, the early march-
          es , the Burntollet ambush, the split with People's Democra-
          cy and the Communist influence in the movement.

          See also : FEENEY, V. E : The civil rights movement in Nor-
                     thern Ireland. (page 69 in this section).

                     KANE, J . J : Civil rights in Northern Ireland.
                     (in this section).

                     SOCIALIST STANDARD : Report from Belfast : The
                     failure of civil rights in Northern Ireland.
                     (in this section).

                     STEWART, Edwina : The present situation of the
                     civil rights movement.
                     (in this section).

                     STEWART, J. D : Civil rights in Ulster.
                     (in this section).

                     HASTINGS, M : Ulster 1969. The fight for civil
                     rights in Northern Ireland. (page 32 in Selec-
                     ted Works Section).

                     EGAN, B & McCORMACK, V : Burntollet (in Pamphlets
                     Section).

                     FARRELL, M : Struggle in the North (in Pamphlets
                     Section).

                     FERMANAGH CIVIL RIGHTS ASSOCIATION : Fermanagh
                     Facts. (In pamphlets section).

                     GREAVES, D : Northern Ireland : Civil rights and
                     political wrongs. (In Pamphlets section).

HERRING, Ivor J : <u>Ulster roads on the eve of the railway age.</u> c.1800 -
1840.
in <u>Irish Historical Studies.</u> Dublin. Sept.1940. Vol.2 No 6

HEWITT, John : <u>No rootless colonist.</u>
pp. 90 - 95
in <u>Aquarius.</u> Benburb. 1972.

Belfast-born poet John Hewitt analyses the crisis of identity
of many people of Planter stock in Northern Ireland.

HIBERNIA: <u>1971 - Internment - 1974</u> .
8 pages supplement
in <u>Hibernia Magazine.</u> Dublin. August 1974. vol. 38 No 13

A series of articles published on the third anniversary of
the introduction of internment without trial in Northern
Ireland. The supplement also contains the launching of a
campaign to end internment. In December 1974, the editor
of Hibernia Magazine, John Mulcahy, presented the Prime
Minister of Great-Britain, Harold Wilson, with a list of
over 100,000 signatures asking for the end of internment
in Northern Ireland.
Short bibliography.

See also : <u>THE COMPTON REPORT & THE PARKER REPORT</u> (page
8 in Official Publications Section).

FIELDS, Rona : <u>A society on the run.</u>

MacGUFFIN, J : - <u>Internment.</u>

- <u>The Guineapigs</u>

(In Selected Works Section : p.29 ; p.38)

HOGGART, Simon : <u>The Army PR men of Northern Ireland.</u>
pp. 79 - 80
in <u>New Society.</u> London. Oct.11. 1973. Vol.26. No 575

A former correspondent of the daily newspaper <u>The Guardian</u>
in Northern Ireland explains the working of the Press Office of the British Army.

HOLMES, Erskine : <u>Northern Ireland 1973 - A Centre party coalition
Government.</u>
pp. 22 - 24
in <u>Community Forum.</u> Belfast. NICRC. 1972. vol.2. No 2

The chairman of the Northern Ireland Labour Party indicates
the direction in which he would like to see the political
centre in Northern Ireland develop.

HOLMES, Erskine : <u>Political possibilities for the people of Northern
Ireland.</u>
pp. 72 - 78
in <u>Administration.</u> Dublin. Winter 1972. Vol.20 No 4

See also : GIBSON, Norman : <u>Political possibilities for the people of Northern Ireland.</u> (Page 70 in this section).

HOLMES , E & THORNTON, A. M : <u>Children in distress : the effects of the disturbances on the pupils in the Ardoyne secondary schools , Belfast.</u>
pp. 29 - 33
in <u>Northern Teacher</u> . Belfast. Summer 1972.

Ardoyne is a Roman Catholic ghetto which has seen much of the present violence.

See also : FRASER, R. M : <u>Children in Conflict.</u> (page 30 in Selected Works Section).

<u>Psychiatric sequelae of the 1969 riots.</u>

<u>Ulster's children of conflict.</u>
(In this section : p.69 - 70)

HOWTON, Hugh : <u>In the streets of broken glass.</u>
pp. 19 - 23
in <u>Soldier</u>. London. June 1971. Vol. 27 . No 6

The riot-torn streets of Ulster as seen by a soldier of the British Army.

See also : BARZILAY, David : <u>The British Army in Ulster.</u>

BARZILAY, D & MURRAY, M : <u>Four months in winter.</u>
(Page 20 in Selected Works Section).

HUME , John : <u>John Hume's Derry.</u>
in <u>Everyman</u>. Benburb. 1970. No 3

Text of a film documentary shot by Radio Telefis Eireann and directed by the Social Democratic & Labour Party Member of Parliament John Hume whose constituency is in the Roman Catholic ghetto of Londonderry.

HUNTER, R. J : <u>An Ulster Plantation town - Virginia.</u>
pp. 43 - 51
in <u>Breifne</u>. Dublin. 1970. vol.4

JACOBSON, Philip : <u>Ulster - The weapons of urban warfare.</u>
pp. 30 - 35
in <u>The Sunday Times Magazine</u>. April 9, 1972.

Descriptions and drawings of the weapons used by the terrorists and the British Army in Ulster.

JAMISON, David : <u>Local Government in Belfast.</u>
in <u>Local Government Review</u> : London.

Part 1 . Vol. 136 No 26 . May 13, 1972
Part 2 . Vol. 136 No 29. June 3, 1972

The Northern Ireland local government was reorganized between 1969 and 1973. The new system came into operation on September 1, 1973.

See also <u>The Macrory Report</u> (Page 8 in Official Publications
Section).

JENKINS, Robin : <u>Religious conflict in Northern Ireland.</u>
pp. 103 - 108
in <u>A sociological yearbook of religion in Britain.</u> London.
1969.

Essential reading.

JENVEY, Sue : <u>Sons & Haters : Ulster Youth in Conflict.</u>
in <u>New Society.</u> London. July 20, 1972.

A penetrating study of " Tartan gangs " , Protestant youths
between 12 & 18, wearing tartan scarves and blue denim out-
fits, fighting on a purely sectarian basis.
The author argues that usually there is hostility between
adolescents and their parents but in Ulster, event the
" Tartan gangs " parallel the adults' own conflicts.
Essential reading.

See also : HOLMES, E & THORNTON , A. M : <u>Children in distress.</u>
(page 76 in this section).

JOHNSTON,Stewart : <u>Serious eye injuries caused by the civil disturbances in Belfast.</u>
pp. 72 - 77
in <u>The Ulster Medical Journal.</u> Belfast. 1971. Part 1. vol 40

Most of these injuries are caused by stones or " rubber bullets " fired by the British Army.

JONES, E : <u>The distribution and Segregation of Roman Catholics in
Belfast.</u>
pp. 167 - 189.
in <u>Sociological Review.</u> London. 1956.

Valuable article.

JONES, W. R : <u>England against the celtic fringe : a study in cultural
stereotypes.</u>
pp. 155 - 171
in <u>Journal of World History.</u> London. 1971. Vol. 13.

KANE, John J : <u>Civil rights in Northern Ireland.</u>
pp. 54 - 77
in <u>Rev. Pol.</u> 1971. vol 23

See also : HEATLEY, Fred : <u>The civil rights story.</u>(page 74
in this section)

KAYE, Jacqueline : <u>The Irish prisoners.</u>
in <u>New Society.</u> London. Sept.6.1973

The author is Secretary of the Prisoners' Aid Committee. This
association is asking for ' political ' status for Irish political prisoners in Great - Britain.

KELLY, Henry : <u>Northern Ireland : so far.</u>
in <u>Eire-Ireland.</u> St Paul (Minnesota) 1971. Vol.6. No 4

A leading Irish journalist on the staff of the daily newspaper <u>The Irish Times</u> reports on the situation in Northern
Ireland since 1968.

KELLY, Henry : <u>Northern Ireland : Beginning or End</u> ?
pp. 39 - 45
in <u>Eire - Ireland.</u> St Paul (Minnesota) . Spring 1972.
vol.7 No 1

See previous entry.

KENDLE, John : <u>Federalism & the Irish problem in 1918.</u>
pp. 207 - 30
in <u>History.</u> London. 1971. vol.56

Valuable article. Federalism is a solution which is advocated by every generation in Ireland.

See also : FENNELL, D : <u>Sketches of the New Ireland.</u>

SINN FEIN (Kevin ST) : <u>Eire Nua.</u>
(In Pamphlets section).

KENNEDY, Henry S : <u>Riot at Lancaster Street.</u>
pp. 99 - 105
in <u>Aquarius.</u> Benburb. 1972.

An eye-witness account by a journalist of the fierce 1935
riots in Belfast.

See also : <u>FOR MEMBERS OF PARLIAMENT.</u>

BOYD, A : <u>Holy war in Belfast.</u>
(page 19 in Selected Works Section and page
22)

BOYD, A : <u>Belfast riots 1935</u> .
(page 63 in this section).

KINGSTON, William : <u>Northern Ireland - The elements of a solution.</u>
pp. 201 - 211
in <u>Political Quaterly.</u> London. April - June 1972. vol.43 No 2

KIRK, T : <u>A sense of community : Park. Co. Londonderry.</u>
pp. 19 - 23
in <u>Community Forum.</u> Belfast. NICRC. 1973. vol.3. No 3

A sociological investigation of a small village in Northern
Ireland.

LAKEMAN, Enid : <u>Proportional Representation in Northern Ireland.</u>
pp.8 - 10
in <u>Community Forum.</u> Belfast. NICRC. 1971. Vol.1. No 2

A leading authority on PR analyses the implications of possible reversion to PR in Northern Ireland. Proportional Represen-

tation was reintroduced for the local government elections on
May 30, 1973 and for the Northern Ireland Assembly elections
on June 28, 1973.

See also : KNIGHT, J & BAXTER-MOORE, N : Northern Ireland
Local Government Elections : 30 May 1973.
(page 2 in Bibliographies and reference works
Section).

ELLIOTT, S : Northern Ireland's election : The
Assembly's heritage.
(page 67 in this section).

KNIGHT, J : Northern Ireland - The elections of
the Twenties. (In pamphlets section).

KNIGHT, J : Northern Ireland. The elections of
1973. (in pamphlets section).

LEAVY, James : Structure or process ? New approaches to the problem of
Northern Ireland.
pp. 107 - 122
in Studies. Dublin. Summer 1973. Vol.62. No 246

A valuable analysis of the different solutions applied to the
Irish Question by the British Government since 1968.

LYONS, F. S. L : The Irish Unionist Party and the devolution crisis of
1904 - 1905.
pp. 1 - 22
in Irish Historical Studies.1948. Dublin. vol.6

Essential reading for detailed research.

LYONS, H. A :Psychiatric sequelae of the Belfast riots.
in The British Journal of Psychiatry.March 1971. Vol.118
No 544.

See also : FRASER, R. M : Psychiatric sequelae of the 1969
Belfast riots. (page 69 in this section).

LYONS, H. A : The Psychiatric effects of civil disturbance.
pp. 17 - 20
in World Medecine. April 21, 1971.

LYONS, H. A : The psychological effects of the civil disturbances on
children.
pp. 35 - 38
in Northern Teacher. Belfast. Winter 1973 .

See also : FRASER, R. M : Children in Conflict.(page 30 in
Selected Works Section).

LYONS, H. A : Psychiatric sequelae of the Belfast riots.
in British Journal of Psychiatry. London. March 1971.

MACAULAY, Ambrose : <u>Catholics in the North. Survey of a century</u>. 1870 - 1970.
pp. 21 - 32
in <u>The Newman Review</u>. Belfast. 1970. Vol.2. No 1

Essential reading.
See also : KENNEDY, D : <u>Catholics in Northern Ireland</u>.1926 - 1939. (page 53 in Relevant Chapters Section).

MACAULAY, Ambrose : <u>The Government of Ireland Act, 1920. The origins of partition</u>.
pp. 289 - 296
in <u>Capucin Annual</u>. Dublin. 1971. vol.38

See also : FAIR, J.D: <u>The Anglo-Irish treaty of 1921</u>. (page 68 in this section).

MACDERMOTT, Lord : <u>The decline of the rule of law</u>.
pp. 474 - 495
in <u>Northern Ireland Legal Quarterly</u>. Belfast. Winter 1972. Vol. 23 No 4

Text of a lecture given by the Lord Chief Justice of Northern Ireland in 1972 on the law and the troubles.

McELROY, Rev. A.H : <u>Ulster Tories responsible for Ian Paisley</u>.
pp. 19 - 25
in <u>New Outlook</u>. London. July / August 1966. No 56

The author is President of the Ulster Liberal Party.

Mac EOIN, Gary : <u>The Irish Republican Army</u>.
pp. 3 - 29
in <u>Eire-Ireland</u>. St Paul (Minnesota). Summer 1974. Vol.9 , No 2

Brief introduction to the subject.

See also : BOWYER BELL, J : <u>The Secret Army</u>.

COOGAN, T : <u>The IRA</u>.
(p.22 & p.25 in Selected Works Section).

McKEOWN, Michael: <u>Civil unrest secondary schools' survey</u>.
pp. 39 - 42
in <u>The Northern Teacher</u>. Belfast. Winter 1973.

Summary of a questionnaire sent to secondary schools in Northern Ireland.

McPHERSON, Mary : <u>Londonderry : learning under fire</u>.
p. 6
in <u>Times Educational supplement</u>. London. Sept.1971. No 2939.

The stress of schoolchildren in Londonderry, the second city of Northern Ireland to endure severe bombing.

MACY, Christopher : <u>The religious factor in Ulster</u>.
       pp. 5 - 9
       in <u>Humanist</u>. London. Jan.1972. Vol.87. No 1

MACY, Christopher : <u>Job discrimination in Northern Ireland</u>.
       pp. 17 - 18
       in <u>Humanist</u>. London. Jan.1972. Vol.87. No 1

MACY, Christopher : <u>Sinn Fein and the IRA's</u> . Part 1. pp. 19 - 20
                                     Part 2. pp. 21 - 23
       in <u>Humanist</u>. London. Jan. 1972. Vol.87. No 1

       In part 1 the author interviews Joe Cahill, then Brigade
       Commander of the Belfast Provisional IRA.
       In part 2 the author examines the split in Sinn Fein and
       concludes that it reflects the sectarian nature of poli-
       tics in Ireland as a whole.

MANSERGH, Nicolas : <u>The Government of Ireland Act.1920 : its origins</u>
<u>& purposes. The working of the ' official ' mind</u>.
       pp. 19 - 63
       in <u>Historical Studies</u>. 1974. Blackstaff Press. vol.9.

       Essential reading.

       See also : BARRINGTON, D : <u>Council of Ireland in the Consti-</u>
                   <u>tutional context</u>. (page 59 in this section).

MANSFIELD, Frank : <u>Focus on Northern Ireland</u>.
       pp. 623 - 638
       in <u>Municipal Journal</u>. London. May 5, 1972. Vol.80.No 18

MARSHALL, William : <u>Council of Ireland in the Context of Europe</u>.
       pp. 18 - 27
       in <u>Administration</u>. Dublin. Winter 1972. Vol.20. No 4

       The concept of the Council of Ireland was originated with
       the Government of Ireland Act 1920.

MULVENNA, Joesph : <u>Internment what now</u> ?
       pp. 93 - 96
       in <u>Aquarius</u>. Benburb. 1974.

       The author was chairman of a study group set up to examine
       the problem of internment.

       See also : HIBERNIA : <u>1971 - Internment - 1974</u>. (page 75
               in this section)

NEW OUTLOOK : <u>Ulster</u>. (Special issue)
       <u>New Outlook</u>. A radical quarterly. London. 1972. No 1. 52 p.

NEWE, Dr. G. B : <u>Whither Ireland now</u> ?
       pp. 66 - 69
       in <u>Aquarius</u>. Benburb. 1974.

       A former Roman Catholic Minister in a Unionist Cabinet at

Stormont examines some propositions put forward by politicians as solutions to the Northern conflict.

NEWSWEEK : <u>The children of violence.</u>
pp. 12 - 18
in <u>Newsweek</u>. (European edition). April 19.1971.

See also : FRASER, R. M : <u>Children of conflict</u>. (page 30 in Selected Works Ssection).

NOLAN, Sean : <u>The Communist Party of Ireland.</u>
pp. 184 - 189
in <u>Marxism Today</u>. London. June 1973. Vol.17. No 6

The Communist Party of Ireland was formed in 1921, then banned and reformed in June 1933.

NOWLAN, Dr.David : <u>Last community link in Ulster, the family doctor.</u>
pp. 9 - 12
in <u>World Medecine</u>. Oct.6. 1971. Vol.7. No 1.

NUSIGHT : <u>Crisis in the North.</u>
pp. 25 - 66
in <u>Nusight Magazine</u>. Dublin. Sept.1969.

The first background analysis published in Ireland, a fortnight after the riots of August 1969.

NUSIGHT : <u>A Profile of Reverend Ian Paisley.</u>
pp. 10 - 12 & 77
in <u>Nusight Magazine</u>. Dublin. Oct.1969

See also : DUDLEY EDWARDS, O : <u>A look at Reverend Ian Paisley.</u>
(page 67 in this section).

MARRINAN, P : <u>Paisley : Man of wrath</u>. (page 40 in Selected Works Section).

NUSIGHT : <u>The phenomenon of Paisleyism</u> .
pp. 13 - 15
in <u>Nusight Magazine</u>. Dublin. Oct.1969.

See also entries mentioned above.

NUSIGHT : <u>The Churches during the crisis.</u>
pp. 37 - 40
in <u>Nusight Magazine</u>. Dublin. Oct.1969.

The author concludes this article : " the era of clerical hegemony in Catholic political circles ended with the advent of the Civil Rights Association."

O'BRIEN , Conor Cruise : <u>Ireland and Minority Rights.</u>
pp. 433 - 435
in <u>Humanist</u>. London. March 1973. Vol.88. No 11

O'LEARY, Cornelius : The Northern Ireland crisis.
pp. 255 - 268
in Political Quarterly. London. July / Sept. 1971. Vol.42 No 3

Essential reading.

O'LOGHLEN, B. A : The patterns of public expenditure in Northern Ireland
and the Republic. 1954 - 1965.
pp. 119 - 144
in Journal of the statistical & social inquiry society of Ireland. Dublin. Vol.21. Part 6 (1967 - 68).

Essential reading for detailed research study.

O'RIORDAN, Michael : The White Paper on Northern Ireland.
pp. 171 - 175
in Marxism Today. London. June 1973. Vol.17. No 6

The General Secretary of the Communist Party of Ireland discusses the Constitutional proposals for Northern Ireland
published by the British Government on March 20, 1973 (See
also : Northern Ireland Constitutional proposals. page 10
in Official Publications Section).

OBSERVER : The weapons of urban warfare.
pp. 30-35
in The Observer Magazine. London. April 9, 1972.

Descriptions and drawings of the weapons used by the terrorists in Ulster.

See also : JACOBSON, Philip ; Ulster - The weapons of urban
warfare.

PAISLEY, Rev. Ian : The case against ecumenism.
pp. 14 - 15
in Community Forum. Belfast. NICRC. 1971. Vol.1. No 1

The Rev. Ian Paisley has always been one of the strongest
opponent of ecumenism in Northern Ireland.

See also next entry.

PRO MUNDI VITA : The Irish Conflict & Christian Conscience . A special
Report.
pp. 554 - 580.
in The Furrow. London. Sept.1973.

RAFTERY, A : Britain & Ireland in the Common Market.
pp. 189 - 191
in Marxism Today. London. June 1973. Vol.17. No 6

The author is editor of the Irish Socialist.
Ireland and Great Britain became members of the EEC on January 1st, 1973.

RANKIN, H. D : <u>On the psychostasis of Ulster.</u>
pp. 160 - 174
in <u>Psychotherapy & Psychosomatics.</u> London. 1971. Vol.19

A penetrating analysis of the incorporation by Ulster Protestants of Irish myths systems and forms.
Essential reading despite specialized vocabulary.

See also : WRIGHT, F : <u>Protestant ideology and politics in
Ulster.</u> (in this section).

REDMOND, Tom : <u>The forces in the Irish national liberation struggle.</u>
pp. 167 - 175
in <u>Marxism Today.</u> London. June 1973. Vol.17 .No 6

The author is the Dublin area Secretary of the Communist
Party of Ireland.

REDMOND, Tony : <u>A sense of community : Broughshane (Co.Antrim).</u>
pp. 23 - 27
in <u>Community Forum.</u> Belfast. NICRC. Vol.3. No 3. 1973

A sociological survey of a small town.

REES, Merlyn : <u>The future of Northern Ireland.</u>
pp. 33 - 37
in <u>Contemporary Review.</u> London. June 1973.

The author was a Labour Shadow Minister of State for Northern
Ireland. He became Secretary of State for Northern Ireland in
Harold Wilson 's Cabinet in March 1974.
Merlyn Rees concludes his article : " The way forward is throu-
gh co-operation between the North & the South of Ireland. "

See also next entry.

REES, Merlyn : <u>Northern Ireland 1974.</u>
in <u>Contemporary Review.</u> London. February 1974.

An analysis of the future of the Province where power-sharing
between the two communities is essential to ensure peace, according to the author.

RICE, Rodney : <u>The North in the Sixties - A personal report.</u>
pp. 71 - 74
in <u>Nusight Magazine.</u> Dublin. Dec.1969.

Essential reading.

ROBERTS, David A. : <u>The Orange Order in Ireland : A religious institution ?</u>
pp. 269 - 282
in <u>The British Journal of Sociology.</u> Sept.1971. Vol.22 No 3

Essential reading.
See also : GRAY, Tony : <u>The Orange Order.</u> (^Page 31 in Selected Works Section).

ROBINSON, A : Londonderry. Northern Ireland : A Border Study.
          pp. 208 - 221
          in Scottish Geographical Magazine. Edinburgh. Dec.1970.

ROSE, Paul : The Northern Ireland Problem .Part 1
          pp. 230 - 233
          in Contemporary Review. London. Nov.1971.

          The author is a Labour MP and was Chairman of the Campaign
          for Democracy in Ulster until March 1973.

ROSE, Paul : The Northern Ireland Problem. Part 2
          pp. 284 - 288
          in Contemporary Review. London. Dec.1971.

          See also : REES, Merlyn : The future of Northern Ireland.
                                    Northern Ireland 1974.
                     (page 84 in this section).

ROSE, Richard : Ulster : the Problem of Direct Rule.
          pp. 498 - 499
          in New Society.London. June 1971. No 454

          The author of Governing without consensus (see page 43 in
          Selected Works Section) analyses what problems would face
          the British Government in case it would suspend the Parlia-
          ment of Northern Ireland and administer the Province from
          London.
          The British Prime Minister, Edward Heath, announced on March
          24, 1972 that the Northern Ireland Parliament was prorogued
          and that the Province was placed under " Direct Rule " of
          Westminster.

ROSE, Richard : Discord in Ulster.
          pp. 122 - 127.
          in New Community. Jan.1972. Vol.1.No 2

ROSE, Richard : After the Cameron Report.
          in New Society. London. Sept.18, 1969.

          The author, who is Professor of Politics at the University
          of Strathclyde, asks if Proportional Representation intro-
          duced in the Northern Ireland Constitution could help to
          create a coalition.

          See also : THE CAMERON REPORT (page 6 in Official Publica-
                     tions Section)

                     LAKEMAN, E : Proportional Representation in
                     Northern Ireland. (pages 78 & 79 in this
                     section).

RUSSELL, James : Violence & the Ulster schoolboy.
          in New Society. London. July 1973. No 564

          Survey showing that Ulster schoolbiys often approve the poli-
          tical violence around them.

See also : RUSSELL, J : <u>Some aspects of the civil education of secondary schoolboys in Northern Ireland.</u> (In Pamphlets Section).

SAVAGE, D. C : <u>The Parnell of Wales has become the Chamberlain of England : LLoyd George and the Irish Question.</u>
pp. 86 - 108
in <u>Journal of British Studies.</u> London.Vol.12. (Symposium : Ireland and British Politics . 1914 - 1921. Part 1).

See also : CURRAN, J. M : <u>Lloyd George and the Irish settlement. 1921 - 1922.</u> (Page 65 in this section).

SAVAGE, D. C : <u>The origins of the Ulster Unionist Party. 1885 - 1886.</u>
pp. 185 - 208
in <u>Irish Historical Studies.</u>Dublin. March 1961. Vol.12

Essential reading.
See also : HARBINSON, J : <u>The Ulster Unionist Party. 1882 - 1973.</u> (page 32 in Selected Works Section).

SCOTT, Roger : <u>The 1970 British General Election in Ulster.</u>
pp. 16 - 32.
in <u>Parliamentary Affairs.</u> London. Winter 1970-1971. No 24

The June General Elections saw the return of a Conservative Government at Westminster and the election, as MP, of the Rev. Ian Paisley.

SIMMS, J. G : <u>Donegal in the Ulster plantation.</u>
pp. 386 - 393
in <u>Irish Geography.</u>Dublin. 1972. Vol.6. No 4

The Government of Ireland Act of 1920 split the historical province of Ulster, awarding counties Donegal, Cavan & Monaghan to the Irish Free State.

SIMMS, J. G : <u>Remembering 1690.</u>
pp. 231 - 242
in <u>Studies.</u> Dublin. Autumn 1974. Vol.251

Remembering 1690 is an old Ulster custom. The author examines why there is a cult of the Battle of the Boyne . He traces its development from the Williamite revolution to the present day and the annual celebration of the Twelfth in Northern Ireland by Orangemen.
Essential reading.
See also : GRAY, Tony : <u>Besieged,betrayed...and bewildered.</u> (page 71 in this section)

WRIGHT, F : <u>Protestant ideology and politics in Ulster .</u> (In this section).

SIMPSON, J.V : <u>The economics of the North's Options.</u>
in <u>Management.</u> London. Sept.1974. Vol.21. No 9

The author examines the financial aspects of the three

options for Northern Ireland : total integration with the
UK, an independent Northern Ireland and a federal Ireland.

See also : GIBSON, N : Political possibilities for the people of Northern Ireland. (Page 70 in this section).

GIBSON, N : Economic and Social implications of
the political alternatives that may be open to
Northern Ireland. (In Pamphlets section).

SINCLAIR, Betty : Trade Unions in Ireland.
pp. 181 - 184
in Marxism Today. London. June 1973. Vol.17. No 6

The author is the Secretary of the Belfast Trade Council.She
was one of the speakers at the civil rights rally in Duke St,
Londonderry, on October 5; 1968 which was dispersed by the
RUC.

See also : BOYD, A : The rise of the Irish trade unions.
(Pages 22-23 in Selected Works Section).

SOCIALIST STANDARD : Report from Belfast : the failure of civil rights
in Northern Ireland.
in Socialist Standard. London. Oct.1969. Vol.65. No 781

The Socialist Standard is the official journal of the Socialist Parties of Great-Britain and Ireland.

See also : HEATLEY, Fred : The civil rights story.
(page 74 in this section).

SNODDY, Oliver : From the Bridge to the Abyss.
pp. 315 - 350
in Capucin Annual. Dublin. 1972. vol.39

An analysis of the articles of agreement for the Treaty of
1921 between Ireland and Great-Britain.

See also : LONGFORD, Lord : Peace by Ordeal.(page 37 in
Selected Works Section).

SPENCER, A.E.C.W : Urbanisation and the problem of Ireland.
pp. 82 - 90
in Aquarius. Benburb. 1974.

A sociological analysis of urbanisation and the present communal conflict in Ireland.

STEED, G.P.F & THOMAS, M.D : Regional Industrial change : Northern Ireland.
pp. 344 - 360.
in Annals of the Association of American Geographers. 1971.

STEWART, Edwina : The present situation of the civil rights movement.
pp. 176 - 180
in Marxism Today. London. June 1973. Vol.17. No 6

See also : HEATLEY, Fred : <u>The civil rights story</u>. (page 74
in this section).

Edwina Stewart is a member of the National Executive Committee
of the Communist Party of Ireland and a leader of the Northern
Ireland Civil Rights Association.

STEWART, James : <u>The roots of socialism in Ireland.</u>
pp. 161 - 166
in <u>Marxism Today.</u> London. June 1973. Vol.17. No 6

The author is Assistant General Secretary of the Communist
Party of Ireland.

STEWART, John D : <u>Civil rights in Ulster.</u>
pp. 13 - 14
in <u>Humanist.</u> London. Jan.1972. Vol.87. No 1

The author, a well-known Ulster journalist, was a founder
member of the Northern Ireland Civil Rights Association.
Here he outlines why this organization was founded.

See also : HEATLEY, Fred : <u>the civil rights story.</u>(page 74
in this section).

THOMAS, M. D : <u>Manufacturing industry in Belfast, Northern Ireland.</u>
pp. 175 - 196
in <u>Annals of the Association of American Geographers.</u> 1956.

ULTACH : <u>The persecutions of catholics in Northern Ireland.</u>
pp. 161 - 175
in <u>Capucin Annual.</u> Dublin. 1940

The author is probably Ambrose Macaulay (see page 80 in this
section).
This article is a strong attack against the Unionist Government of Northern Ireland.

Essential reading.

See also : ULTACH : <u>The Orange Terror.</u> (In Pamphlets Section)

WAGHORN, J. H : <u>Civilianisation of the Royal Ulster Constabulary.</u>
pp. 423 - 424
in <u>Local Government Chronicle.</u> March 13, 1971.

See also : <u>The Hunt Report</u> (Page 6 in Official Publications
Sections).

WALLACE, Martin : <u>Disintegrating Unionism.</u>
in <u>Eire-Ireland.</u> St Paul. Minnesota. Vol.5. No 2.

A study of the reactions of the Unionists faced with civil
rights demands.

See also : WALLACE, M :-<u>Drums & Guns - Revolution in Ulster.</u>
-<u>Northern Ireland - 50 years of self-
Government.</u>(Page 45 in Selected
Works Section).

WATSON, Alex : <u>Liberal watershed.</u>
    pp. 8 - 9
    in <u>Community Forum</u> . Belfast. NICRC. 1973. Vol.3. No 1

    A study of PACE (Protestant & Catholic Encounter) one of
    the numerous peace movements of Northern Ireland.

WEINER, R.S.P & BAYLEY, John : <u>British troops and Ulster's political</u>
    <u>leaders.</u>
    in <u>New Society</u>.London. Aug.20, 1970.

    Over 60 political leaders in Ireland were interviewed and
    asked questions about the physical intervention of Britain
    in Northern Ireland and the progress of the Stormont reform
    programme. The survey was carried out in 1969.

    Essential reading.

WHALE, John : <u>Modern guerilla movements.</u>
    pp. 3 - 6
    in <u>Community Forum</u>. Belfast. NICRC. 1973. Vol.3. No 2

    The author, main correspondent in Northern Ireland for the
    British sunday newspaper <u>The Sunday Times</u>, shows that the
    IRA offensive in Ulster can be regarded as part of a world-
    wide phenomena.

WHYTE, John H : <u>Whitehall ,Belfast & Dublin : a new light on the Treaty</u>
    <u>and the Border.</u>
    pp. 233 - 242
    in <u>Studies</u>. Dublin. 1971. Vol.60.

    A review article of <u>Whitehall Diary: Vol.III</u> by T.S Jones.
    (See page 34 in Selected Works Section).

WILSON, Fr. Desmond : <u>The Northern Ireland situation.</u>
    in <u>The Newman review</u>. Belfast. 1969. Vol.1. No 2

WILSON, Fr. Desmond : <u>The Sixties the years of opportunity.</u>
    pp. 7 - 16
    in <u>Aquarius</u>. Benburb. 1973.

    An analysis of the religious situation in Northern Ireland in
    the sixties and what might have happened without the troubles.

    See also : PAISLEY, Rev.Ian : <u>The case against ecumenism.</u>
                (page 83 in this section).

WINCHESTER, Simon : <u>As other see us - The United States.</u>
    pp. 6 - 8
    in <u>Community Forum</u>.Belfast. Vol.4. No 1 . 1974.

    The author is now correspondent in the United States for the
    British daily newspaper <u>The Guardian</u>. Previously he reported
    from Northern Ireland.

    See also : WINCHESTER, S : <u>In holy terror</u>. (Page 46 in Selec-
                ted Works Section).

WINDLESHAM, Lord : <u>Ministers in Ulster : the machinery of Direct Rule.</u>
pp. 261 - 272
in <u>Public Administration.</u> Journal of the Royal Institute of
Public Administration. London. Autumn 1973. Vol.51

This article is a revised version of a lecture given at the
New University of Ulster on April 26, 1973.
Lord Windlesham was Minister of State in the Northern Ireland Office from March 26, 1972 to June 5,1973. Here he analyses the problems involved in dealing with the running of
the Province with its legislative and executive powers
transferred to the UK Parliament and to a British Minister.

See also : ROSE, Richard : <u>Ulster - The Problem of Direct</u>
<u>Rule.</u> (page 85 in this section).

WRIGHT, Frank : <u>Protestant ideology and politics in Ulster.</u>
pp. 213 - 280
in <u>European Journal of Sociology.</u> 1973. Vol.14.

The author analyses the ideologies of the Ulster protestant
community, the beliefs they hold about the Roman Catholic
minority in Northern Ireland and the relation between these
beliefs and the solidarity the Protestants generally display
in opposing any Roman Catholic participation in political
power.
This is probably one of the best studies ever made so far on
the subject.
It covers from the Plantations time to 1973.

See also : EVANS, E.E : <u>The personality of Ireland.</u>

SIMMS, J.G : <u>Remembering 1690.</u>

PAISLEY, Rev.I : <u>The case against ecumenism.</u>

GRAY, T : <u>Besieged,betrayed and bewildered.</u>

ROBERTS, D.A : <u>The Orange Order in Ireland : A</u>
<u>religious institution</u> ?

(In this section : p.68 ; p.86; p.83; p.71 ; p.84)

8 - PAMPHLETS

COMMENTARY UPON THE WHITE PAPER Cmd 558 entitled ' A RECORD OF CONSTRUC-
TIVE CHANGE.
1971. Belfast. Irish News. 39 p.

This pamphlet was written by a group of Roman Catholics who
had resigned from public bodies after the introduction of
internment on August 9. 1971. They claimed that few practical
effective reforms had been made by the Northern Ireland government over the previous 2 years.

See also : A record of constructive change.(page 8 in Official
Publications Section).

ALLIANCE PARTY OF NORTHERN IRELAND : 34,000 new jobs. A call for self
help in industry and employment from the Alliance Party of
Northern Ireland.
June 1972. Belfast. 11 p.

A plan to fight unemployment which " still remain 7,5 % overall "
according to the pamphlet.

ARDOYNE EX-RESIDENTS ASSOCIATION : Ardoyne - The true story. Foreword by
Hugh Stockman.
n.d (c.1973). Belfast. 18 p.

This work argues that " republican arsonists " burned out the
houses of Farringdon Gardens in Belfast during internment week
in August 1971.

See also : MacGuffin, J : Internment ! (page 38 in Selected
Works section).

ASSOCIATION FOR LEGAL JUSTICE : Torture - The Record of British Brutality
in Ireland.
n.d (c.1971). Belfast. ALJ & Northern Aid. 39 p.

This work contains mainly signed statements of men arrested by
the security forces during internment week in August 1971.
The Association for Legal Justice was formed in Belfast on
April, 25, 1971. It fights for legal rights of persons arrested
and for reforms in the legal system in Northern Ireland.

See also : MACGUFFIN, J : Internment !
The Guineapigs.
(Page 38 in Selected Works Section - See also there
entries related to internment and detention).

BARRITT, D. P & BOOTH, A : Orange & Green - A quaker study of community
relations in Northern Ireland.
1972. Sedbergh (Yorkshire). Northern Friend's Peace Board.71 p.

One of the best short and unbiased introduction on this complex
subject.

See also : BOOTH, A (ed.) : <u>Orange & Green</u> (in this section)

BARRITT, D & CARTER, C : <u>The Northern Ireland Problem</u>. (Page 19 in Selected Works Section)

BELFAST LIBERTARIAN GROUP : <u>Ireland, dead or alive</u> ? An analysis of Irish politics.
n.d (c.1973). Belfast. 24 p.

An analysis of the present situation in Ireland by a group of libertarian socialists.

BENNETT, Jack : <u>The Northern Conflict & British Power</u>.
1973. Dublin. The Irish Sovereignty Movement. Pamphlet No 1. 20 p.

A Belfast journalist of Protestant background and a founder member of the Northern Ireland Civil Rights Association asks for self-determination so that Protestants and Roman Catholics can run " their own country ".

See also : BENNETT, J : <u>Introduction</u> (in <u>Freedom the Wolfe Tone Way</u>. See page 48 in Relevant chapters Section).

BENNETT, Jack : <u>Fourteen days of fascist terror, in Northern Ireland</u>.
1974. London. Irish Democrat Book Centre . 20 p.

This work deals with the Loyalist strike organized by the Ulster Workers Council from May 15 to May 29, 1974. It brought down the first Northern Ireland Executive where power was shared bewteen Roman Catholics and Protestants. Immediately the British Government reintroduced Direct Rule for the Province from Westminster.

BIGGS-DAVIDSON , John : <u>Catholics and the Union</u>.
Introduction by G. B. Newe.
1972. Belfast. Unionist Research Department. 16 p.

A British Conservative MP gives a controversial analysis of the attitude of ⁴rish Roman Catholics towards the Union with Great Britain since 1800.

See also : BIGGS-DAVIDSON, J : <u>The Hand is Red</u>. (Page 20 in Selected Works Section.)

BLACK, Richard and FRANCIS, Pinter and OVARY, Bob : <u>Flight</u>. <u>A report on population movement in Belfast during August 1971</u>.
1971. Belfast. NICRC. 20 p.

According to this report, 2,000 families left their homes, involving a shift of 10,000 people. Conclusions are suggested about the patterns of population movements in Belfast.
Maps. Essential reading.

See also : MACGUFFIN, J : <u>Internment !</u> (Page 38 in Selected Works Section)

ARDOYNE EX-RESIDENTS ASSOCIATION : <u>Ardoyne - The
True Story</u> (page 91 in this section).

BLADES, Michael & SCOTT, Dominic : <u>What price Northern Ireland</u> ?
1970. London. Fabian Society. 24 p.

The authors recommend more British Government involvement
in the Province's economy.
Valuable statistics.

See also : <u>Northern Ireland :Finance & the Economy</u>. (Page 12
in Official Publications Section).

BLEAKLEY, David : <u>Crisis in Ireland.</u>
1974. London. Fabian Society. 32 p.

The author argues that the present situation in Northern
Ireland makes the province vulnerable to the threat of
fascism. He calls for the application of Labour's social
policies (a massive programme of social and economic
reconstruction) and for the development of community
government (but not coalition government) based on
getting existing religious divided sectarian groups to
rule together .

See also : BLEAKLEY, D : <u>Peace in Ireland.</u> (Page 21 in Selected Works Section).

BOAL, F. W & DOHERTY,P & PRINGLE,D. G : <u>The spatial distribution of
some social problems in the Belfast urban area</u>.
1974. Belfast. NICRC. 132 p.

A 2 year study in human need, sickness and family breakdown
in the Belfast area.
Maps, notes and statistics.
Essential reading for detailed research.

See also : BOAL, F. W in Articles Section, page 61.

BOGSIDE REPUBLICAN APPEAL FUND : <u>Battle of Bogside</u>.
1969. Belfast. 49p.

A pictorial history of the street battles in the Roman Catholic Bogside district of Londonderry on August 12, 13, 1969.

See also : LIMPKIN, C : <u>The Battle of the Bogside</u>.

STETLER, R : <u>The Battle of the Bogside</u>.

(In Selected Works Section : p.36; p.44)

BOOTH, A (ed.) : <u>Orange & Green.</u>
A quaker study of community relations in Northern Ireland.
1969. Sedbergh (Yorkshire). Northern Friends' Peace Board.
51 p.

The first edition of this work. For a second and revised edition see : BARRITT, D. P & BOOTH, A : <u>Orange & Green</u>. (Page
91 in this section).

BOW GROUP (Ulster Section) : <u>Local Government in Ulster - A new</u>
<u>organization structure.</u>
1969. London. Bow Group. 20 p.

The Bow Group is an association linked to the British Conservative Party.
Reforms in local government were one of the main demands of
the civil rights movement.

BOYD, Andrew : <u>The Two Irelands</u> .
1968. London. Fabian Society. 27 p.

See also : BOYD, A : <u>Holy war in Belfast.</u> (page 22 in Selected Works section).

BRITISH & IRISH COMMUNIST ORGANISATION :

This organisation was previously known as the Irish Communist
Organisation and took its name of British & Irish Communist
Organisation in 1970.
It is in a unique position as a Stalinist body which upholds
the distinctiveness of a Protestant Ulster.

<u>The Economics of Partition.</u>
1969. Cork. ICO. 51 p.
1972. Belfast. B & ICO. Revised and extended edition. 83 p.

<u>The Birth of Ulster Unionism.</u>
1970. Cork. B & ICO. 44 p.

See also: BUCKLAND, P : <u>Ulster Unionism and the origins of</u>
<u>Northern Ireland.</u> (Page 16 in Gene-
ral Works).

HARBINSON, J : <u>The Ulster Unionist Party.1882 -</u>
<u>1973.</u> (Page 31 in Selected Works
Section).

<u>The People's Democracy. From a working class viewpoint.</u>
1970. Cork. B & ICO. 31 p.

See also : ARTHUR, P : <u>The People's Democracy.</u>(Page 19 in
Selected Works Section)

<u>The Two Irish Nations - A reply to Michael Farrell.</u>
1971. Belfast. B & ICO. 39 p.

An answer to the leader of the ᴾeople's Democracy who had at-
tacked the two nations theory as formulated by the B & ICO.

See also : WORKERS ASSOCIATION : <u>One island, two nations.</u>
(In this section).

<u>The Home Rule Crisis. 1912 - 1914.</u>
1971. Belfast. B & ICO. 64 p.
1972. Belfast. B & ICO. Second and revised edition. 76 p.

See also : STEWART, A.T.Q : <u>The Ulster Crisis</u>. (Page 44 in
                                  Selected Works Section).

<u>Article 44. The historical background to constitutional
change in Southern Ireland</u>.
1972. Belfast. B & ICO. 13 p.

On December 8,1972 voters in the Republic of Ireland decided
in a referendum by 721,003 to 133,430 to delete Article 44
of the 1937 Constitution. This article recognised the special position of the Roman Catholic Church in the State.

" Hidden Ulster " explored. A reply to P.O'Snodaigh's " Hidden Ulster ".
1973. Belfast. B & ICO. 50 p.

This work refutes P.O'Snodaigh's conclusions published in
his pamphlet " Hidden Ulster ". See O'SNODAIGH, P in this
section.

BROCKWAY, Lord : <u>Northern Ireland Bill of Rights</u>.
Text & Explanation - Based & Revised version of Lord Brockway's Bill of Rights in 1971.
n.d (c.1973). London. Connolly Publications. 11p.

The author wants to use the British legal system of law to
protect the Roman Catholic minority of Northern Ireland. At
the present the Province has no Bill of Rights and several
organisations and personalities have been asking for one.
Lord Brockway presented several times his project at Westminster but it was always rejected.
Lord Brockway was a speaker at the march organised by NICRA
in Londonderry on January 30, 1972 when 13 civilians were
killed by the British Army.

BUCKLAND, Patrick : <u>Irish Unionism</u>.
1973. London. The Historical Association. 48 p.

A concise but very useful essay which explains Irish Unionism.
Short bibliography and sound chronological account. This
work is a good introduction to Buckland's volumes on the
subject.

See also : BUCKLAND, P : <u>The Anglo-Irish & the new Ireland</u>.

                           <u>Ulster Unionism & the origins of
                           Northern Ireland</u>.

                           <u>Irish Unionism. A documentary history</u>.
            (Page 16 in General Works Section).

BURNS, Elinor : <u>British Imperialism in Ireland</u>. A marxist historical
         analysis.
         1931. Dublin. Workers Book. 66 p.
         1974. Cork. Cork Workers Club. (Second and unabridged edition)

         See also : STRAUSS, E : <u>Irish Nationalism & British Democracy</u>.
                           (Page 18 in General Works Section).

CALVERT, Harry : <u>The Northern Ireland Problem</u>.
        1972. London. United Nations Association. 15 p.

        The author is Professor of Law at the University of Newcastle-upon-Tyne. He was for a time a consultant to the Northern Ireland Government. He was an adviser to Brian Faulkner, Chief Executive Designate, at the Sunningdale Conference in December 1973.

        See also : CALVERT, H : <u>Constitutional Law in Ireland</u>.(Page
                                 24 in Selected Works Section).

CAMPAIGN FOR SOCIAL JUSTICE IN NORTHERN IRELAND : <u>The Plain Truth</u>.
        1969. Dungannon. (second edition). 35 p.

        From the introduction : This booklet attempts to explain the situation in Northern Ireland, and to detail the discriminatory injustices from which the minority has been suffering for almost 50 years.
        Valuable statistics - Essential reading.

        The Campaign for Social Justice in Northern Ireland was founded in January 1964 by Dr.Con & Mrs Patricia McCluskey in order to collect and publicise the facts of discrimination done by the Ulster Unionist Government against the Roman Catholic minority.

CAMPAIGN FOR SOCIAL JUSTICE IN NORTHERN IRELAND : <u>Northern Ireland -
The mailed fist : a record of army and police brutality
from August 9 to November 9,1971</u>.
        1972. Dungannon. CSJNI & ALJ. 71 p.

        With a foreword by Tony Smythe, Secretary of the National Council for Civil Liberties.
        This work contains signed statements by internees.

        See also : MacGUFFIN, J : <u>Internment !</u>

                        <u>The Gineapigs</u>.
                        (Page 38 in Selected Works Section).

CAMPBELL, J. J : <u>Catholic schools - A survey of a Northern Ireland
Problem</u>.
        n.d (c. 1962). Belfast. 40 p.

        See also : AKENSON, D. H : <u>Education & Enmity</u> .(Page 19 in
                          Selected Works Section).

                CONWAY, Cardinal : <u>Catholic schools.</u> (In this
                              Section).

CATHERWOOD, Sir Frederick : <u>Christian duty in Ulster today</u>.
        1970. London. Evangical Press.

        The author is a former Director-General of the British National Economic Development Council from 1966 to 1971.

See also : CATHERWOOD, Sir F.: A possible settlement of the
Northern Ireland Problem.(Page 49 in Relevant
Chapters Section).

CENTRAL CITIZEN'S DEFENCE COMMITTEE (BELFAST) :
The true story - Terror in Northern Ireland.
1969. Dublin. 19 p.

This pamphlet is based on signed statements taken from eye-
witnesses of the rioting during the summer 1969. It also
examines the actions of the Northern Ireland Government
during that period.

See also : The Cameron Report ; The Scarman Report.(Pages 6
and 9 of the Official Publications Section).

Northern Ireland - The Black Paper - The Story of the Police.
1973. Belfast. CCDC. 41 p.

This document highlights the need for an acceptable police
system as the basic preliminary to a solution of the problem of Northern Ireland. It denies that the reforms set
down by the Hunt Report were ever implemented.

See also : The Hunt Report. (Page 6 in Official Publications
Section).

CLANN NA hEIREANN : The Littlejohn memorandum. The true story of British
and Irish espionage services active in Ireland.
1974. London. Clann na hEireann. 34 p.

A study of the activities of the Littlejohn Brothers. In October 1972 they were arrested and jailed in Dublin for a bank
robbery. The claimed to have been working all the time for
British intelligence in Ireland to discredit the IRA. In August 1973 they were sentenced by a Dublin Court to 20 and 15
years penal servitude. In early 1974, Kenneth Littlejohn
escaped from a Dublin jail. At the end of the year he was
recaptured by British police in Great-Britain.

COMMUNIST PARTY OF IRELAND:
The Stormont elections - A working class analysis.
n.d (c.1960). Belfast. 10 p.

The situation in the North.
Aug.1969. Belfast. 6 p.

The crisis in the Unionist Party.
1969. Belfast. 14 p.

A democratic solution. Programme adopted 15th national congress.
Belfast 16-17, 1971.
n.d (c.1971). Belfast. 26 p.

COMMUNITY RELATIONS , Ministry of :
Schemes of assistance for persons affected by civil disturbances.
1973. Belfast. Ministry of Community Relations. 20 p.

This pamphlet deals with compensations for criminal injuries,
involvement of security forces,bomb and riot damage,housing,
intimidation,etc...

CONWAY, Andy : There are no evil men... A fresh look at the Irish Question and a suggestion way forward.
1972. Dublin. New Ireland Movement. 30 p.

This is an answer to the NUM pamphlet " Two Irelands or One ? "
(See in this section).
According to the author no one is to blame for the present
situation :" all people of this island were trapped by their
shared reactionary conflict born out of segregation ".
He proposes a new all-Ireland constitution, with a series of
referenda in Northern Ireland and in the Republic of Ireland.

CONWAY, Cardinal William : Catholic Schools.
1971. Dublin. Veritas Publications. 18 p.

Cardinal Conway, Archbishop of Armagh and Primate of All
Ireland, rejects that segregated schooling as it is practised
in Northern Ireland is the cause of division in the Province
and argues that Protestant families would not agree to " mixed
schooling ".

See also : CAMPBELL, J.J : Catholic schools. (Page 96 in this
section).

CORKEY, Rev.William : Episode in the history of Protestant Ulster .
1923 - 1947.
n.d. Belfast. 152 p.

The author is a Presbyterian and tells a " story of the
struggle of the Protestant community to maintain Bible ins-
tructions in their schools ".

See also entry above.

CORRIGAN, Aidan : Eye-witness in Northern Ireland.
n.d (c.1970). Dungannon. 37 p.

An account of the events of 1969.

See also : Central Citizen's Defence Committee: The true story
Terror in Northern Ireland. (Page 97 in this
section).

CRAIG, William : The future of Northern Ireland.
1972. Belfast. Vanguard Publications. 10 p.

William Craig MP is a former Minister for Home Affairs (from
October 1966 to December 1968) in the Northern Ireland

Government. He founded Ulster Vanguard on February 9, 1972 and described it as a political organisation being an " umbrella for traditional Unionist groupings with the aim of rallying all loyalists."
This pamphlet is a statement on behalf of the United Loyalist Council, representing Ulster Vanguard, the Loyalist Association of Workers, the Ulster Defence Association and Loyalist Defence Volunteers. It is an answer to the British Government's Green Paper published on October 30, 1972.

See also : The future of Northern Ireland : A Paper for Discussion. (Pages 9 & 10 in Official Publications Section).

CRONIN, Sean : The rights of man in Ireland.
1970. Dublin. Dublin Wolfe Tone Society. 32 p.

See also : CRONIN, S : Ireland since the Treaty.
(Page 26 in Selected Works Section).

CROZIER, Brian (ed.) : Ulster : Politics and terrorism.
1973. London. Institute of Conflict Studies. Conflict Studies No 36. 20 p.

This work puts forward the view that the security situation in Northern Ireland had improved and political institutions within the Province's framework would enable some sort of peace to emerge.

See also : CROZIER, Brian & MOSS, Robert (editors): The Ulster Debate.(Page 26 in Selected Works Section).

DARBY, John & MORRIS, Geoffrey : Intimidation in Housing.
1974. Belfast. NICRC. 117 p.

This work was completed in Spring 1973 but publication was delayed as findings were thought to be controversial by the authorities. This report analyses the flight of Roman Catholic and Protestant families from riot-torn districts of Belfast following intimidation.

Maps, notes. Essential reading.

See also : BLACK, R & FRANCIS, P & OVARY, B : Flight.
(Page 92 in this section).

DASH, Samuel : Justice Denied - A Challenge to Lord Widgery's Report on " Bloody Sunday ".
1972. New - York. The Defence & Education Fund of the International League for the Rights of man. 85 p.

This pamphlet includes the full report of Lord Widgery (See page 9 in Official Publications Section).
This work contains evidence challenging the official British report on the shooting of 13 civilians in Londonderry on January 30, 1972 by British troops.
The author is Director of the Institute of Criminal Law &

Procedure of GeorgeTown University Law Center.

DASH, Samuel : <u>Justice Denied - A Challenge to Lord Widgery's Report</u>
        <u>on " Bloody Sunday ".</u>
        1972. London. The Defence & Education Fund of the Interna-
        tional League for the Rights of Man in association with the
        National Council of Civil Liberties. 48 p.

        This is the British version of Professor Dash's report (see
        entry mentioned above) which does not contain Lord Widgery's
        report.

DEVLIN, Paddy : <u>Tuzo, Whitelaw and the Terror in Northern Ireland.</u>
        1973. Belfast. Published by the author. 55 p.

        The author, a Roman Catholic, was elected in February 1969
        to represent the Falls Constituency of Belfast (a Roman
        Catholic district) at the Stormont Parliament. He became
        later the Chief Whip of the SDLP and was Minister of Health
        and Social Services in the Northern Ireland Assembly Execu-
        tive in 1974.
        In this collection of articles he analyses British policy
        in Northern Ireland and argues that the Roman Catholic com-
        munity is terrorised by the British Army while Orange mili-
        tants are appeased.

DEWAR, Rev. M.W : <u>Why Orangeism ?</u>
        1959. Belfast. Orange Order of Ireland. 24 p.

        A concise description and history of the movement with a
        chapter on " The points at issue between Protestantism &
        Roman Catholicism."

        See also : DEWAR, BROWN & LONG : <u>Orangeism : a new his-</u>
                        <u>torical appreciation.</u> (Page 27 in Selected
                        Works Section).

DORN, Robert : <u>Irish nationalism and British Imperialism.</u>
        1973. Dublin. Revolutionary Marxist Group. 55 p.

DUGGAN, G. C : <u>Northern Ireland - Success or failure ?</u>
        1950. Dublin. Irish Times. 42 p.

        The author was a Comptroller Auditor-General for Northern
        Ireland. This is an edited series of informative articles
        which appeared in the <u>Irish Times</u> newspaper in April 1950.

        Essential reading.

DUGGAN, G. C : <u>A United Ireland.</u>
        1954. Dublin. Irish Times. 24 p.

        A series of 9 articles reprinted from the <u>Irish Times</u>.
        The author examines some of the practical questions implicit
        in the case of reunion.
        Essential reading.

EGAN, Bowes & McCORMACK , Vincent : <u>Burntollet.</u>
   1969. London. LRS Publications. 64 p. / (Second edition.
   1969. 68 p.)

   This work retraces the events of the People's Democracy march
   from Belfast to Londonderry on January 4,1969 when students
   were ambushed by militant Protestants near Burntollet Bridge
   in County Londonderry.
   Essential reading.
   See also : DEVLIN, B : <u>The Price of My soul</u>. (Page 27 in Se-
      lected Works Section).

      <u>The Cameron Report</u>. (Page 6 in Official Publica-
      tions Section).

FABIAN SOCIETY : <u>Emergency Powers : a fresh start.</u>
   1972. London. Fabian Society. 31 p.

   This is the work of an informal group of Queen's University
   Law students (in Belfast) drafted under the chairmanship
   of W.L.Twinning, Professor of Law. It looks at the problems
   of public order in an emergency and analyses the Special
   Powers Act of 1922 applied in Northern Ireland only. It also
   proposes a new Emergency Powers Security Act for the whole
   of the United Kingdom with additional safeguards for any
   individual.

   Essential reading.

   See also : NARAIN, B. J : <u>Public law in Northern Ireland</u>.
      (Page 41 in Selected Works Section).

FARRELL, Michael : <u>Struggle in the North.</u>
   1969. London. Pluto Press. 34 p.
   1972. London. People's Democracy. (Second edition). 37 p.

   A socialist analysis of the situation in Northern Ireland
   by the leader of People's Democracy with emphasis on the
   civil rights movement and the part played by Dublin politicians.

FARRELL, Michael : <u>The great eel robbery.</u>
   1970. Belfast. People's Democracy. 24 p.

   In September 1970 the People's Democracy started to challenge
   the fishing rights on Lough Neagh belonging to the Chichester-
   Clark family since 1661. The Lough is famous for its eels.
   Following agitation and strikes, on January 27, 1972, the Toome
   Eel Fishery Company formally handed over the eel fishing rights
   on Lough Neagh to the Lough Neagh Fishermen's Co-operative
   Society.

   Essential reading.

   See also : HEALY, T : <u>The great Fraud of Ulster</u>. (Page 33 in
      Selected Works Section).

FARRELL, Michael : <u>The Battle for Algeria</u>.
      1973. Belfast. People's Democracy. 16 p.

      The author argues that the algerian struggle is relevant to
      understand the Northern Ireland situation.

FARRELL, Michael : <u>Behind the Wire</u>.
      1974. Belfast. People's Democracy. 40 p.

      This is a collection of articles about life in Belfast's
      Crumlin Road Jail and Long Kesh internment camp since 1971.
      Michael Farrell was arrested on August 9, 1971 then freed
      and later emprisoned from June 26,1973 to August 8,1973.

      See also : HIBERNIA : <u>1971 - Internment - 1974</u>.(Page 75 in
              Articles Section).

              MacGUFFIN, J : <u>Internment</u>. (Page 38 in Selected
              Works Section).

FAUL, Fr. Denis & MURRAY, Fr. Raymond :
      <u>British Army and Special Branch RUC Brutalities. Dec.1971 -
      Feb.1972</u>.
      n.d. (c.1972) .Cavan. 78 p.

      A collection of signed statements from persons arrested by
      the security forces.

      <u>Whitelaw's Tribunals . Long Kesh Internment camp. Nov.1972 -
      Jan. 1973</u>.
      n.d (c.1973). Dungannon. 46 p.

      This pamphlet deals with the judicial powers and the Deten-
      tion of Terrorists (Northern Ireland) Order introduced on
      November 7,1972 and the Diplock Report published on Decem-
      ber 20, 1972.

      See also : <u>The Parker Report & the Compton Report</u>. (Page 8
              in Official Publications Section).

      <u>The iniquity of Internment. 9th August 1971 - 9th August 1974</u>.
      n.d (c.1974). Dungannon. 31 p.

      See also : HIBERNIA : <u>1971 - Internment - 1974</u>. (Page 75 in
              Articles Section).

      <u>The Hooded Men. British Torture in Ireland. August-October 1971</u>.
      1974. Dungannon. 129 p.

      A history of internment and interrogation since 1971. It also
      deals with the numerous effort of several organisations to
      end internment and contains detailed accounts of interrogation .

      See also : MacGUFFIN, J : <u>The guineapigs</u> .(Page 38 in Selec-
              ted Works Section).

      <u>The Flames of Long Kesh</u>.
      1974. Dungannon.

A detailed account of the burning of the internment camp
outside Belfast and of the revolt of Republican prisoners
there in October 1974.

FENNELL, Desmond : <u>Sketches of the New Ireland</u>.
1973. Galway. Association for the advancement of self-government. 27 p.

The author advocates a new system of local government based
on the " regions " grouped under Provincial Parliaments
and a central Government in Athlone. This is a proposal
very similar to the Provisional Sinn Fein plan.

See also : SINN FEIN PROVISIONAL : <u>Eire Nua</u>. (In this
section).

McMANUS, F : <u>Ulster : The Future</u>. (In this
section).

FERMANAGH CIVIL RIGHTS ASSOCIATION : <u>Fermanagh Facts</u>.
n.d (c. 1969). Enniskillen. Fermanagh CRA. 35 p.

This pamphlet details gerrymandering, religious and politi-
cal discrimination of Roman Catholics in employment in
County Fermanagh. It also covers the discrimination in
housing.
Essential reading.
See also : CAMPAIGN FOR SOCIAL JUSTICE IN N.I : <u>The Plain
Truth</u>. (Page 96 in this section).

FOLEY, Gerry : <u>Ireland in Rebellion</u>.
1971. New - York. Pathfinder Press. 31 p.

A marxist analysis which includes interviews with Cathal
Goulding, Chief of Staff of the Official IRA and Thomas
McGiolla, President of Official Sinn Fein.

FOLEY, Gerry : <u>Problems of the Irish Revolution. Can the IRA meet
the challenge ?</u>
1972. New - York. Pathfinder Press. 31 p.

FOX, Ralph : <u>Marx, Engels and Lenin on the Irish Revolution</u>.
1932. London. Modern Books. 36 p
1974. Cork. Cork Workers Club. (Second edition)

GALLAGHER, Eric : <u>A better way for Irish Protestants and Roman Catholics</u>.
Advice from John Wesley.
1973. Mission Board of the Methodist Church in Ireland. 14 p.

The author is Chairman of the Mission Board of the Methodist
Church.

GANNON, Jack : <u>Catholic political culture & the Constitution of Ireland</u>.
1971. Belfast. B & ICO. 82 p.

This analysis applies only to the Republic of Ireland. Appendix 2 shows the considerable emotion in the island about the choice of names used for it and for its different parts.

See also : B & ICO : <u>Article 44 . The historical background to constitutional change in Southern Ireland.</u> (Page 95 in this section).

GARDNER, Louis : <u>Resurgence of the majority.</u>
n.d (c. 1970). Belfast. Ulster Vanguard. 44 p.

An analysis of the Ulster situation in terms of Unionists and Republicans seeing the conflict in terms of national affiliations. It hardly mentions the Roman Catholic Church at all. The author was full time Secretary of the Ulster Vanguard Movement from May 4, 1972 to Octobre 22, 1972.

Essential reading to undertsand the loyalist point of view.

GIBSON, Norman (ed.) : <u>Economic and social implications of the political alternatives that may be open to Northern Ireland.</u>
1974. Coleraine. The New University of Ulster. 81 p.

Essential reading. Valuable statistics.

This booklet contains 5 papers presented at a conference held at the New University of Ulster on November 1, 2, 1974. The participants at the conference included politicians from all the parties represented in the prorogued Northern Ireland Assembly, except the parties constituting the United Ulster Unionist Council (Official Unionist Party, Ulster Vanguard and Democratic Unionist Party.

Chap.3 : A comparison of economic and social conditions in Northern Ireland and the Republic of Ireland.

This chapter provides some factual background material as a basis from which to consider the economic and social implications of three political alternatives : Northern Ireland as part of the United Kingdom, an independent Northern Ireland and a Federal Ireland.

Chap.4 : Northern Ireland as part of the UK (by C.F.Carter).

This paper considers two main alternative forms of being part of the UK : a " county " solution and a " Stormont " solution .

Chap.5 : An independent Northern Ireland (by T.Wilson).

This paper considers the controversial and difficult topic of an independent Northern Ireland. This polical alternative has been advocated , at different periods, by the Ulster Vanguard Party, the Official Unionist Party and the members of the Ulster Workers Council.

Chap.6 : Some economic implications of a federal Ireland (by B.R. Dowling).

This paper examines the economic implications of a
Federal Ireland, a political alternative suggested
by Provisional Sinn Fein and some Protestant leaders
such as John Taylor and Desmond Boal.

See also : GIBSON, N : Page 70 in Articles Section .

CROZIER, B & MOSS, R : The Ulster Debate.(Page
26 in Selected Works Section).

NORTHERN IRELAND : FINANCE & ECONOMY (Page 12
in Official Publications Section).

GILLIES, Rev. Donald : In place of truth.
1973. Belfast. Unionist Publicity Department. 36 p.

The author has been minister in the Protestant area of the
Shankill Road and Clifton St in Belfast, scene of many riots.
He argues that there has been too much propaganda against
the Protestant community hiding the truth.about the situation in the Province.

GILMORE, George : The Irish Republican Congress.
1935. New - York. 25 p.
1974. Cork. Cork Workers Club. (Second edition.) 27 p.

An important document concerning a turning point in the
history of the Irish Republican Army.
In April 1934 at Athlone, a conference of IRA men , disa-
greeing with the IRA Army Convention , and radical organisations issued a manifesto. The signatories asserted their
belief that " A Republic of a united Ireland will never be
achieved except through a struggle which uproots capitalism
on its way " and asked for a Congress. It was held in Autumn
1974 and in all effect split the IRA down the middle.

See also : BOWYER BELL, J : The Secret Army

COOGAN, T : The IRA.
(In Selected Works Section : p.22; p.25)

GREAVES, Desmond : The Irish Question and the British People : a plea
for a new approach.
n.d (c.1963). London. Connolly Publications. 33 p.

GREAVES, Desmond : How to end Partition.
1949. Ripley. Connolly Association. 15 p.

GREAVES, Desmond : The Irish Case against Partition : Full facts &
programme of action.
1961. London. (?). 36 p.

GREAVES, Desmond : Northern Ireland : Civil rights and political
wrongs.
1969. London. Communist Party. 11 p.

See also : HEATLEY, F : The civil rights story. (Page   74
in Articles Section).

GREER, John : A Questioning Generation.
          1972. Belfast. Church of Ireland Board of Education. 88 p.

          A report on 6th Form religion in Northern Ireland.
          Valuable survey. Essential reading.

          See also : ITA : Religion in Britain & Northern Ireland.(In
                    this section).

HADDEN, Tom & HILLYARD, Paddy : Justice in Northern Ireland. A study
          of social confidence.
          1973. London. Cobden Trust. 74 p.

          A lawyer and a lecturer in social administration give examples
          of judicial bias against Roman Catholics.

          See also : PROSECUTIONS IN N.I : A STUDY OF FACTS. (page 11
                    in Official Publications Section)

HAMILTON, Iain : The Irish Tangle.
          1970. London. Institute for the Study of Conflict. Conflict
          Studies No 6. 18 p.

          Valuable introduction to the subject (see especially the
          Essential Data section).
          The author concludes his study by writing : " The events
          set in train 5 years ago by the first meeting of Captain
          Terence O'Neill and Sean Lemass have ensured that the ques-
          tion of reunification can wait no longer on time and good-
          will alone."

HAMILTON, Iain & MOSS, Robert : The spreading Irish Conflict .
          1971.London. Institute for the Study of Conflict. Conflict
          Studies No 17. 27 p.

          This work includes two articles.
          In the first, Iain Hamilton provides an analytical narrative
          of recent events,against the historical background, and in-
          cludes an attempt to isolate the causes of the deteriora-
          tion since 1968.
          In the second article Robert Moss analyses the security si-
          tuation in Ulster in the light of the capabilities of the
          opposing forces.

HARWOOD, Jeremy & Others : Ireland - Our Cuba ?
          1970. London. Monday Club. 13 p.

          J.Harwood, J.Guinness and John Biggs-Davison, members of the
          right-wingMonday Club show the part played by left-wing ele-
          ments in the Northern Ireland crisis.

HAWKINS, John : The Irish Question today.
          1941. London. Fabian Society & Gollancz. 53 p.

INDEPENDENT TELEVISION AUTHORITY : Religion in Britain and Northern Ire-
          land.
          1970. London. ITA. 56 p.

This survey made in February 1968 in Britain and in January
1969 in Northern Ireland contains extremely valuable data.

See also : GREER, J : A questioning generation. (Page 106
in this section).

INSIDE STORY : Northern Ireland (Special Issue).
1972. London. Inside story. 35 p.

This special issue of a left-wing magazine contains unsigned
articles describing the censorship of the British Press cove-
ring Northern Ireland.

See also : McCANN, E : The British Press & Northern Ireland.
(In this section).

IRISH REPUBLICAN ARMY, OFFICIAL : In the 70's the IRA speaks.
1970. London (?). A Repsol pamphlet. 20 p.

The programme of the new IRA following the end of the campaign in the North in February 1962.
Essential reading to understand the civil rights movement
and the Official IRA policy and campaign since 1966.

IRISH REPUBLICAN ARMY, PROVISIONAL : Freedom struggle by the Provisional
IRA.
1973. Dublin (?) . 101 p.

Most copies of this booklet,explaining the present campaign &
policies of the Provisional IRA,were seized at the printers
in Drogheda on July 4, 1973 by the Irish Police. It was later
reprinted in Britain. It contains also a roll of honour of
men who have died since 1969 and the proposals for a federal
Ireland.
Essential reading.

JACKSON, Harold : The Two Irelands : a dual study of inter-group tensions.
1971. London. Minority Rights Groups. 25 p.
1972. (Revised edition).

A former journalist on the staff of the British daily The
Guardian provides a brief but detailed handbook of the present conflict.

KENNALLY, Danny & PRESTON, Eric : Belfast ,August 1971 : a case to be
answered.
1971. London. Independent Labour Party. 124 p.

This report was prepared by members of the National Adminis-
trative Council of the Independent Labour Party (I.L.P) at
the request of the SDLP and members of the NICRA.
It examines'the evidence relating to the treatment of detainees, the harassment, intimidation and brutality of the British Armed forces towards the Catholic Community, and the living conditions of the Catholic people with particular reference to the circumstances surrounding evictions.'

It contains mainly signed statements and there is a chapter on the British Army .

See also : MacGUFFIN ,J : The Guineapigs.

Internment.
(Page 38 in Selected Works Section).
FAUL, Fr.D & MURRAY, Fr.R : Page 102 in this section)

KERR, Rev. W. S : Slanders on Ulster, reply to the " Orange Terror ". 1944. Belfast. Ulster Unionist Council. 8 p.

See ULTACH : The Orange Terror .(In this section).

The author was the Dean of Belfast.
In this short work he denies any of the evidence provided by Ultach in his strong attack against Unionist Governments in Northern Ireland.
Essential reading, it shows the role of propaganda in the Northern Ireland conflict.

KNIGHT, James : Northern Ireland - The Elections of the Twenties : The General Election for the House of Commons of the Parliament of Northern Ireland : May 1921 & April 1925 .
By the system of proportional representation by the single transferable vote in multi-member constituencies & May 1929 by the X - vote in single-member constituencies.

1972, London. Arthur MacDougall Fund. 54 p.

Valuable collection of results and an analysis of the PR system in Northern Ireland.

See also : LAKEMAN, E : Proportional Representation in Northern Ireland.
(Pages 78-79 in Articles Section).

KNIGHT, James : Northern Ireland - The elections of 1973. 1974.London. Arthur McDougall Fund. 77 p.

Detailed results of the elections for the Northern Ireland Assembly held in June 1973.

See also : ELLIOTT, S : Northern Ireland's elections : The Assembly Heritage. (Page 67 in Articles Section).

LEE, Gordon & TAYLOR, Robert : Ulster - A survey by the ' Economist '. 1971. London. The Economist. 34 p.

An updated reprint of a special survey published in the British financial weekly The Economist on the 50th anniversary of Northern Ireland.

See also : THE ECONOMIST : Ulster - A special survey. (Page 67 in Articles Section).

LINDSAY, Kennedy : The Ulsterman's guide to the White Paper.
1973. Belfast. Ulster Vanguard Publications. 17 p.

The author, who became an Assembly Member in the Northern Ire-
land Assembly, attacks the proposals contained in the British
" White Paper " entitled " Northern Ireland Constitutional
Proposals " (See page 10 in Official Publications Section)
published on March 20, 1973. They outline the scheme for a
Council of Ireland.

LINDSAY, Kennedy : Dominion of Ulster.
1972. Belfast. Ulster Vanguard Publications. 19 p.

From the text : " On the northern approaches to Europe there
is room for an Ulster - independent, democratic, flexible, ima-
ginative and deeply British ".

LONG, Michael : Ulster - The case for regionalisation.
1973. Belfast. Ulster Unionist Party. 24 p.

The author explains the desirability and the liability of a
regional assembly in Northern Ireland, following the introduction of Direct Rule from Westminster in 1972.

LONGFORD, Lord : Forty years of Anglo-Irish relations.
1958. Cork University Press. 16 p.

A valuable survey. This is the text of an address delivered
at University College, Cork, on December 11, 1957.

McCANN, Eamonn : The British Press & Northern Ireland.
1971. London. Northern Ireland Socialist Research Centre. 28 p.

In this socialist analysis, the author argues that the British press is censored and has been publishing " propaganda "
on the North.
Essential reading.

See also : WINCHESTER, S : In holy terror. (Page 46 in Selected Works Section).

McCANN, Eamonn : What happened in Derry ?
1972. London. Socialist Worker Pamphlet. 15 p.

This pamphlet is based on eye-witness accounts, unpublished
newspapers articles and one the author's personal involvement
in the events of January 30, 1972 in Londonderry when 13 civilians were shot dead by the British Army.

See also : The Widgery Report (Page 9 in Official Publications Section).

DASH, Samuel : Justice Denied (Page 99 in this
section).

McGARRITY, J : Resistance - The story of the struggle in British-Oc-
cupied Ireland.
1957. Dublin. Irish Freedom Press. 120 p.

The name ' McGarrity ' is probably a pseudonym.
This book covers the period from the Anglo-Irish Treaty to
1957. The author also explains why the IRA started a new
" Campaign of Resistance in Occupied Ireland " on December
12, 1956. The campaign ended on February,22,1962 after being
called to a halt by the Army Council of the IRA.

McINERNEY, Michael : <u>Trade unions bid for peace in North</u>.
1970. Dublin. Irish Times. 23 p.

This series of articles reprinted from the <u>Irish Times</u> asses-
ses among other topics the position of the trade unions and
labour movement in the North and describes the battle of the
Protestant and Roman Catholic union shopstewarts in Belfast
shipyards and elsewhere to prevent the August 1969 riots from
spreading.

See also : SINCLAIR, B : <u>Trade-Unions in Ireland</u>. (Page 87
in Articles Section).

BOYD, A : <u>The rise of the Irish Trade-Unions</u>.
(Page 22 in Selected Works Section).

McKEOWN, Michael : <u>The first five hundred</u>.
1972. Belfast. Published by the author. 23 p.

A detailed analysis of the first five hundred victims in Northern Ireland since 1969 and how they died. This work also
shows the increase in sectarian assassinations during 1972.

Essential reading for detailed research.

See also : DILLON, M & LEHANE, D : <u>Political murder in Northern Ireland</u>. (Page 28 in Selected Works Section).

McLARNON, J & CORKEY, D : <u>A survey of facts, figures and opinion relating to the economic situation in Londonderry</u>.
1971. Belfast. NICRC. 7 p.

McLENNAN, Gordon : <u>Britain and the Irish Crisis</u>.
1973. London. Communist Party. 20 p.

A communist commentary on the ' White Paper ' published by the
British Government on March 20, 1973.

See also : NORTHERN IRELAND CONSTITUTIONAL PROPOSALS (Page 10
in Official Publications Section).

McMANUS, Frank : <u>Ulster : the future</u>.
1972. Cavan. published by the author. 32 p.

The author, Chairman of the Fermanagh Civil Rights Association,
proposes a federal solution to solve the Irish Question.He was
elected MP at Westminster Parliament on June 19, 1970 for the
Fermanagh & South Tyrone constituency.

See also : Sinn Fein Provisional : <u>Eire Nua</u>. (In this section)

FENNELL,D : <u>Sketches of a new Ireland</u>.(Page 103 in
this section).

110

MAGEE , John : <u>The teaching of Irish History in Irish schools.</u>
1971. Belfast. NICRC. 10 p.

This work describes the process by which the different traditions of history became incorporated into schools curricula
North & South of the Border.

Essential reading.

See also : O'BRIEN ,C.C : <u>States of Ireland.</u> (Page 41 in
Selected Works Section).

MALONE, J. M : <u>Schools project in Community Relations.</u>
1972. Belfast. Published by the author. 41 p.

A former headmaster of a secondary school in Belfast investigates the contribution schools might make to improve relations between Roman Catholics and Protestants.

MOLES, T : <u>Ulster Facts & the ' Ulster Legend ' - Statistical ' Disco-
veries '! Amazing misstatements refuted.</u>
n.d (c.1920). Belfast. Ulster Unionist Council. 16 p.

An Ulster MP 'defends' Ulster from the 'attacks' of the
Nationalist minority. A good example of the propaganda war
waged between the two communities in Northern Ireland.

NATIONAL COUNCIL FOR CIVIL LIBERTIES :
<u>Crisis in Northern Ireland</u> :The representations of the Natio-
national Council for Civil Liberties to H.M.Government.
1971. London. NCCL. 22 p.

Essential reading.

<u>Report of a commission of inquiry appointed to examine the pur-
pose and effect of the Civil Authorities (Special Powers)
Acts (Northern Ireland) 1922 & 1933.</u>
1936. London. NCCL. 40 p
1972. London. NCCL (Reprint).

From the conclusions of the Commission : " The Commission...
believes that the operations of the Special Powers Acts has
the most widespread effect upon political life in Northern
Ireland. The existing conditions of rule - secured by the
supercession of representative government and the abroga-
tion of the rule of law and the liberty of the subject,the
bases of Special Powers - cannot be described otherwise than
as totally un-British.
It is clear to the Commission that the way to the re-establish-
ment of constitutional government, the prerequisite of law and
order in democratic communities, can be paved only by the re-
peal of the Special Powers Acts. Wherever the pillars of constitutional rule,Parliamentary sovereignty and the rule of law
are overthrown there exist the essential conditions of dicta-
torship. It is sad that in the guise of temporary and emergency legislation there should have been created under the shadow of the British Constitution a permanent machine of dic-

tatorship - a standing temptation to whatever intolerant or bigoted section may attain power to abuse its authority at the expense of the people it rules ".

Essential reading.

A review of the 1936 NCCL Commisssion of inquiry in the light of subsequent events.
1972. London. NCCL. 20 p.

This is a post-script to the Report of a commission of inquiry appointed to examine the purpose and effect of the Civil Authorities (Special Powers) Acts (Northern Ireland) 1922 & 1933.It is a commentary on the subsequent legislative changes that have affected the situation. The Northern Ireland (Temporary Provisions) Act 1972 radically affected the Northern Ireland Constitution but it did not alter the practical workings of the Special Powers Acts.

Essential reading for detailed research.

See also : Northern Ireland (Emergency Provisions) Act 1973. Chapt.53.
(Page 11 in Official Publications Section).

NEW SOCIETY : Northern Ireland - A New Society social studies reader.
1973. London. New Society. 31 p.

A collection of articles on Ulster since 1969 .

See also Articles Section.

NEW ULSTER MOVEMENT :

This movement was launched on February 6,1969 by Brian Walker. It planned then to provide electoral support for pro-Captain O'Neill - then Prime Minister of Northern Ireland - candidates at the election of February 1969. It is an interdenominational movement.

The Reform of Stormont.
1971. Belfast. NUM. 16 p.

This plan was drafted by Dr.J.Whyte of Queen's University,Belfast. He recommends the introduction of Proportional Representation for parliamentary elections, a system of all party specialist committees in Parliament and an enlargement of the Northern Ireland Parliament by 50 %.

A commentary on the programme of reforms for Northern Ireland.
1971. Belfast. NUM.

Northern Ireland : The way forward.
1971. Belfast. NUM. 12 p.

Northern Ireland & The Common Market.
1972. Belfast. NUM. 15 p.

A plain man's guide to the EEC, suggesting that Northern
Ireland can derive great economic profit.

Two Irelands or one ?
1972. Belfast. NUM. 14 p.

The NUM lists five major obstacles to Irish Unity.

Violence & Northern Ireland.
1972. Belfast. NUM. 16 p.

The movement urges immediate and unconditional talks with the
men of violence.

A new constitution for Northern Ireland.
1972. Belfast. NUM. 10 p.

The NUM suggests power-sharing in a new regional assembly
under the sovereign authority of Westminster.

Ireland - Towards the return of the rule of law.
1973. Belfast. NUM. 14 p.

This is the text of a memorandum sent to the Inter-Party Committee set up by the Dublin Parliament in May 1972 regarding
a united Ireland.

Tribalism or Christianity in Ireland ?
1973. Belfast. NUM. 31 p.

A stimulating analysis of the relationship between Northern
Ireland's problem and the Churches.

NORTHERN IRELAND CIVIL RIGHTS ASSOCIATION :

The NICRA was formed on January 29, 1967 with a charter based
on that of the National Council of Civil Liberties.

Massacre at Derry.
1972. Belfast. NICRA. 48 p.

In this work the NICRA argues that the events of January 30,
1972 were the results of orders from the British Government.
In Londonderry on that day 13 civilians were shot dead by the
British Army. The pamphlet also denies the conclusions of the
Report of Lord Widgery.

See also : Lord Widgery Report .(Page 9 in Official Publica-
                tions Section)

           DASH, S : Justice Denied.(Page 99 in this section.

           McCANN, E : What happened in Derry ?(Page 109 in
                this section).

Proposals for Peace.Democracy and community reconciliation.
1973. Belfast. NICRA. 19 p.

A commentary on the British Government ' White Paper ' published on March,20, 1973.

See also : <u>Northern Ireland Constitutional Proposals.</u>(Page
10 in Official Publications Section).

NORTHERN IRELAND COMMUNITY RELATIONS COMMISSION :

The NICRC was set up in October 1969 and was terminated in August 1974.

<u>First Annual Report.</u>
1971. Belfast. NICRC. 32 p.

<u>Second Annual Report.</u>
1974. Belfast. NICRC. 24 p.

<u>Guide for intimidated families.</u>
June 1974. Belfast. NICRC. 20 p.

Where, how & when intimidated families can get help and relief
from the Northern Ireland authorities.

See also : DARBY, J & MORRIS, G : <u>Intimidation in Housing.</u>
(Page 99 in this section).

NORTHERN IRELAND POLICE AUTHORITY :

<u>The first three years.</u>
1973. Belfast. Police Authority for Northern Ireland. 59 p.

An account of the Royal Ulster Constabulary since the establishment of the Police Authority in 1970 following the publication of the Hunt Report.
Useful statistics about recruiting and violence.

NORTHERN IRELAND SOCIETY OF LABOUR LAWYERS : <u>Discrimination - Pride for
Prejudice.</u>
1969. Belfast. NISLL. 16 p.

This paper advocated law reform in Northern Ireland regarding
incitement to discrimination.

O'BRADAIGH, Ruari : <u>Our people - our future.</u> What ' Eire Nua ' means.
1973. Dublin. Sinn Fein Provisional. (Second enlarged
edition). 60 p.

A collection of articles on the programme of Sinn Fein Provisional by the President of the movement.

O'FEARGHAIL, Sean Og : <u>Law (?) & Orders.</u> The Belfast "Curfew" of 3-5
July 1970.
1970. Dundalk. Dundalgan Press. Published for the CCDC. 45 p.

This pamphlet details the happenings in the Lower Falls area
of Belfast when the British Army GOC NI, Lt-General Sir Ian
Freeland, declared a "curfew". The pamphlet also contains

signed statements of complaints of damage done by troops while searching houses.

The author of the pamphlet is Michael Dolley.

O'SNODAIGH, Padraig : <u>Hidden Ulster</u>. The other hidden Ireland. 1973. Dublin. Clodhanna Teo. 39 p.

The author, the President of the Gaelic League, argues that the Protestant settlers of Ulster assimilated the Gaelic culture and thus he strives to demolish one of the planks of the " Two Nations " theory : that the Irish language is not part of the heritage of the Ulster Protestant community.

See also : B & ICO :"<u>Hidden Ulster</u>" explored.(Page 95 in this section).

WORKERS ASSOCIATION : <u>One island, two nations.</u>(In this section).

O'TUATHAIL, Seamus : <u>They came in the morning.</u> Internment. Monday August 9, 1971. 1971. Dublin. National Book Service. 41 p.

Seamus O'Tuathail gives here a personal account of his arrest by the British Army on Monday 9, 1971. The pamphlet also contains signed statements of other internees.

See also : MacGUFFIN, J : <u>Internment</u>. (Page 38 in Selected Works Section).

<u>HIBERNIA</u> : <u>1971 - Internment - 1974.</u> (Page 75 in Articles Section).

PAISLEY, Rev.Ian : <u>United Ireland - Never</u> ! 1972. Belfast. Puritan Printing Co. 16 p.

<u>Northern Ireland - What is the real situation</u> ? 1970. Bob Jones University Press. Greenville (Sth Carolina). 22p.

Essential reading to understand the Rev.Ian Paisley's policies.

See also : MARRINAN, P : <u>Paisley : Man of wrath</u>. (Page 40 in Selected Works Section).

DUDLEY EDWARDS,O : <u>A look at Reverend Ian Paisley</u>. (Page 67 in Articles Section).

PALLEY, Claire : <u>The evolution, disintegration and possible reconstruction of the Northern Ireland Constitution.</u> 1972. Belfast. B.Rose and the Institute of Irish Studies.(reprinted from the Anglo-American Law Review. May 1972).

See also : NEWARK, F.H : <u>The law & the constitution.</u>(Page 56 in Relevant chapters section).

PATTERSON, Monica : The Hungry Sheep of Ulster.
1974. Belfast. Platform Publications. 80 p.

A Roman Catholic examines the attitude of her Church in Northern Ireland in the light of the recent troubles.
The author was Chairman of the peace movement ' Women Together ' from 1971 to 1973.
Foreword by Fr.Desmond Wilson.

See also : PRESBYTERIAN CHURCH IN IRELAND (See below)

PEOPLE'S DEMOCRACY :

The real Ulster '71.
1971. Belfast. PD. 13 p.

Published as a radical appraisal of Ulster when the Ulster '71 Exhibition was held in Belfast to commemorate the 50th anniversary of Northern Ireland.

See also : SHEARMAN, H : Northern Ireland : 1921 - 1971.
                    (Page 18 in General Works Section)

What it stands for.
1972. Dublin. People's Democracy. 18 p.

The programme of this left-wing movement founded in October 1968 at Queen's University, Belfast.

See also : ARTHUR, P : The People's Democracy. (Page 19 in Selected Works Section).

PRESBYTERIAN CHURCH IN IRELAND :

Religious discrimination in Ireland .
1967. Belfast. Annual Report. PCI. (Revised edition). 11 p.

From the introduction : " This study has been undertaken because we believe that it is the duty of our Church to meet the widespread allegations of religious intolerance which are made about this country."

Church and Community. Part 1 .
January 1969. Belfast. PCI. 4 p.

A statement for the guidance of Church members following the eruption of violence in Northern Ireland.

Church and Community. Part 2.
June 1969. Belfast. PCI. 4 p.

A statement for the guidance of Church members regarding their duties as Christians in the disturbed North.

Radical Change, Reform and Revolution.
1971. Belfast. PCI. 27 p.

A report of the General Assembly of the Presbyterian Church in Ireland analysing the situation in Northern Ireland.

The Northern Ireland situation.
1972. Belfast. PCI. 20 p.

A collection of statements by the Presbyterian Church in Ireland on the Northern Ireland situation, from 1968 to 1972, explaining what action the Church is taking.

Christians in a situation of Conflict.
1973. Belfast. PCI. 13 p.

A report of the committee on national aid and international problems to the General Assembly 1973.
Answers to a questionnaire ' On being the Church in a situation of Conflict ' have been summarised and are presented in this report.

The Northern Ireland situation.
1973. Belfast. PCI. 11 p.

A selection of Church statements from September 1972 to February 1973.

Northern Ireland Constitutional Proposals.
1973. Belfast. PCI. 4 p.

Observations on the British Government's White Paper agreed by the General Board of the General Assembly, 22nd March 1973.

See also : NORTHERN IRELAND CONSTITUTIONAL PROPOSALS (Page 10 in Official Publications Section).

PURDIE, Bob : Ireland Unfree.
1972. London. IMG Publications. 68 p.

A Trotskyite analysis of the Irish Question.

RAFTERY, A : The Exploited Island.   The economic and class background to Ireland's crisis.
1972. Dublin. Communist Party of Ireland. 23 p.

A Marxist analysis with particular emphasis on Northern Ireland.

RED PATRIOT : An Analysis of the significance of the Ulster Workers' Strike - May 14 - 30, 1974 .
1974. Dublin. The necessity for change Institute of anti-imperialist studies. 76 p.

This pamphlet contains a series of articles from the Red Patriot Editorial Staff. This newspaper is the weekly organ of the Communist Party of Ireland - Marxist Leninist.
The Ulster Workers Council called a general strike in Northern Ireland to show their disapproval of the policies of the Northern Ireland Assembly Executive. At the end of the strike, the Executive resigned and Direct Rule was reimposed from Westminster.

See also : WORKERS ASSOCIATION : <u>The Ulster General Strike.</u>
(In this section).

ROBB, John : <u>New Ireland - Sell out or Opportunity ?</u>
1972. Belfast. New Ireland Movement. 50 p.

The author is a surgeon in the Royal Victoria Hospital in
Belfast. Following the bombing of the Abercorn Restaurant
in the city on Saturday March 4, 1972, he gave a radio in-
terview in which he vividly described the injuries he had
seen in the hospital. Two persons were killed and 130 people were hurt in this explosion. There was no warning.

In this pamphlet, John Robb, an Ulster Presbyterian, argues
that Northern Protestants and Roman Catholics should unite
and take the initiative for the eventual re-unification of
Ireland.

Essential reading.

ROBINSON, D. P : <u>The North answers back.</u>
n.d (c.1970). Belfast. 51 p.

The author, Chairman of 2nd Lagan Valley Ulster Protestant
Volunteers, criticizes the Unionist and Westminster Governments and asks if Ulster would have " to go it alone " to
find a solution to its problems.

ROYAL ULSTER CONSTABULARY : <u>Memorandum submitted to the Lord Hunt</u>
<u>Advisory Board.</u>
1969. Belfast. RUC. 12 p.

The memorandum was submitted by the central representative
body of the RUC.
Lord Hunt was appointed on Agust 21, 1969 to inquire into
the structure of the RUC and the USC. He published his report on October 10, 1969.

See also : <u>The Hunt Report.</u> (Pages 6 - 7 in Official Publications Section).

RUSSELL, James : <u>Some aspects of the civic education of secondary</u>
<u>schoolboys in Northern Ireland.</u>
1972. Belfast. NICRC. 31 p. and Appendix.

This report based on a large survey of secondary school children in Northern Ireland provides information about the attitudes of children towards authority and violence.

Essential reading.

See also : RUSSELL, J : <u>Violence and the Ulster schoolboy.</u>
(Page 85 in Articles section).

SHEARMAN, Hugh : <u>How Northern Ireland is governed</u> - Central Government and Local Government in Northern Ireland.
1963. Belfast. HMSO. 31 p.

A brief description .

SHEARMAN, Hugh : Conflict in Northern Ireland.
1972. Belfast. Unionist Research Department. 15 p.

A Unionist analysis of the crisis.

SHEARMAN , Hugh : 27 myths about Ulster.
1972. Belfast. Unionist Research Department. 12 p.

Counter propaganda.

SINCLAIR, Betty : Unemployment .
1973. Dublin. Communist Party of Ireland. 14 p.

A survey of the problem North and South and possible solutions.

See also : ALLIANCE PARTY OF N.I : 34,000 new jobs.(Page 91
in this section).

SINN FEIN, OFFICIAL :

Also known as Sinn Fein Gardiner St.

Ireland - Background to what is happening to day.
n.d (c.1972). Dublin. SF. 18 p.

Essential reading to understand Sinn Fein Gardiner St policies.

Fianna Fail - The IRA Connection .
n.d. (c.1973). Dublin. (No publisher but SF Gardiner is probably the publisher of this anonymous work). 68 p.

This pamphlet claims that the Fianna Fail political party in
Republic of Ireland financed the Provisional IRA.

Essential reading.

SINN FEIN, PROVISIONAL :

Also known as Sinn Fein Kevin St.

Eire Nua. The social & economic programme of Sinn Fein.
1971. Dublin. SF. 54 p.

This programme contains the case for a federal Ireland.

Essential reading.

Ireland : the facts.
1971. Dublin. SF. 24 p.

Bilingual pamphlet (available in French-Italian ; German-Spa-
nish; English-Irish) giving a concise account of the history
of Ireland and the Sinn Fein programme.

Lost Liberties - The Offences against the State Act.
1972. Dublin. SF. 12 p.

On December 3, 1972 the Offences Against the State (Amendment)

Bill became law in the Republic of Ireland. It placed the onus on defendants to prove that they were not members of the IRA.

The Quality of life in the new Ireland.
1973. Dublin. SF. 17 p.

A collection of articles on the social and economic programme of Sinn Fein.

SMYTH, Clifford :

The author, who is a member of the Rev.Ian Paisley's Free Presbyterian Church, was elected to the Northern Ireland Assembly - although it had been prorogued in May 1974 - in a by-election held on June 20,1974. Clifford Smyth belongs to the DUP, the Rev.Ian Paisley's political party.

To be or not to be, that is the question...for Ulster !
1970. Enniskillen. West Ulster Unionist Council. 12 p.

This pamphlet attacks the " law & order " policy of the Unionist Government in Northern Ireland.

Ulster Assailed.
1970. Belfast. Unionist Party. 36 p.

The author argues that the civil rights movement is the " Trojan " horse of left-wing politics.

Ulster must fight.
1972. Belfast. Published by the author. 8 p.

A hard line and staunch Protestant view of the crisis in the North.

The axis against Ulster, the IRA, Eire and the Church of Rome.
n.d. (c.1972) Belfast. Puritan Printing. 24 p.

The author argues that the present crisis in Ulster is a papish plot against Protestantism.

Politics of deception.
n.d. (c.1972). Belfast. Puritan Printing. 13 p.

The author attacks the three Prime Ministers of Northern Ireland (T.O'Neill ; J.Chichester-Clark ; B.Faulkner) who tried to introduce reforms for the minority.

Rome - Our Enemy.
1974. Belfast. Published by the author. 86 p.

From the introduction : " The author trusts that by the time the reader finishes this text it will have become clear that Protestants have every good cause not merely to distrust the Church of Rome but to indict that religious system as the instigator of Irish unrest ". Then the author surveys and analyses the period from 1641 to the present day.

SMYTH, Rev. Martin : <u>In defence of Ulster</u>.
n.d.(c.1969). Belfast. County Grand Lodge of Belfast. 15 p

An Orangeman point of view of the troubles.
The author was appointed Imperial Grand Master of the Imperial Grand Orange Council of the World in July 1973.
Here he asked that " Roman Catholic Church and Hierarchy must learn to recognise all that has been done for them and pay tribute honestly for it ".

SMYTH, Rev. Martin : <u>The Battle for Northern Ireland</u>.
1972. Belfast. County Grand Lodge of Belfast. 24 p.

The author refutes the national aspiration of Roman Catholics and argues that the reunification is a papist machination.
The battle is not only a physical one but also one for the defence of the Protestant faith, according to him.

SMYTH, Samuel : <u>Fight, compromise or fade away - Your choice</u>.
n.d. (c. 1973). Belfast. Published by the author. 9 p.

The author is a founder member of the protestant para-military organisation the Ulster Defence Association. It was formed at the end of August 1971.
Here he argues that the Swiss system of cantons could provide peace in Ireland.
At the end of 1974, Samuel Smyth left the UDA.

SOCIAL DEMOCRATIC & LABOUR PARTY : <u>Towards a new Ireland</u>.
1972. Belfast. SDLP. 15 p.

This is a policy document.It was published simultaneously in Belfast and in Dublin on September 20,1972.
It envisaged a Treaty between the Republic of Ireland and Great Britain and a declaration of intent by the British Government on the eventual unity of Ireland. It also proposes a dual sovereignty over Northern Ireland by both the British Government and the Republic of Ireland.

Essential reading.

SPENCER, A.E.C.W : <u>Ballymurphy - A tale of two surveys. 1971 - 1973</u>.
1973. Belfast. Queen's University Belfast. Department of social studies. 150 p.

Two socio-economic surveys of one of the most troubled areas of Belfast.
Essential reading, statistics.

See also : BOWEN, Desmond : <u>The Ballymurphy estate.</u>
(Page 62 in Articles section)

" ULSTER'S FINANCES " : How dependent is Ulster on Westminster ?
n.d (c.1972). Belfast. Ulster Times. 16 p.

This Unionist pamphlet questions that Northern Ireland is
fundamentally dependent on Westminster for its financial
needs and suggests a dominion status for the Province.

See also : Northern Ireland : Finance & Economy.(Page 12
in Official Publications Section).

GIBSON, N : Economic and social implications of
the political alternatives that may be open to
Northern Ireland.(Page 104 in this section).

ULSTER UNIONIST COUNCIL : America and the Irish Question.
1920. Belfast. UUC. 8 p.

" A short account of the visit of the delegation from Protestant Ireland to the Churches in the USA " - December 1919-
February 1920.

ULSTER UNIONIST PARTY :

Ulster - The facts.
1969. Belfast. UUP. 12 p.

This pamphlet describes " the anatomy of an uprising " during
August 1969. Later Justice Scarman, appointed to investigate
this period said that this publication was " unfortunate in
its authorship and in its timing ".

Must this go on in Ulster ?
1972. Belfast. UUP. 14 p.

An account of the violence since 1969 followed by " The right
to peace - A statement of concern and hope for every law-abi-
ding citizen in Northern Ireland ".

Peace, order and Good Government .
1973. Belfast. UUP. 24 p.

This the manifesto of Brian Faulkner's Unionist Party before
the elections for the Northern Ireland Assembly in June 1973.
The Unionist Party favoured the establishment of a Council of
Ireland providing the Republic of Ireland recognised the status of Northern Ireland and that it should not be used as a
" stage " towards Irish unity.

Essential reading.

ULSTER UNIONIST PUBLICITY DEPARTMENT : Putting people first in housing.
1973. Belfast. UUP. 28 p.

This paper presents a number of suggestions for a better
housing policy in Northern Ireland. Housing has always been
a pressing problem in the province and it was particularly
exacerbated since the beginning of the troubles.
In December 1974, a survey by the Northern Ireland Housing

Executive showed that 20% of the houses were unfit.

ULSTER UNIONIST RESEARCH DEPARTMENT :

PR & Ulster.
n.d.(c.1972). Belfast. UUP. 10 p.

How Proportional Representation works and advice for Unionists, how they should approach the local government elections of 1973.

Ulster, stepping stone for Communism.
1972. Belfast. UUP. 12 p.

Northern Ireland : the hidden truth.
n.d (c.1972). Belfast. UUP. 24 p.

This pamphlet states a certain number of facts to discount propaganda and analyses 50 years of Unionist Government in the province.

Towards the future.
1972. Belfast. UUP. 20 p.

This work contains the Unionist Party's proposals for the future government of Northern Ireland : an executive assisted by five chairmen of committees. The Foreword is by Brian Faulkner, Leader of the Unionist Party.
In January 1974, Brian Faulkner left the Unionist Party - which became the ' Official Unionist Party ' - and launched in April 1974 the ' Unionist Party of Northern Ireland '.

The future of Northern Ireland.
A commentary on the Government's Green Paper.
Nov,1972. Belfast. UUP. 28 p.

This work discusses all the points mentioned in the British Government 's Green Paper and studies in detail the " Irish Dimension " concept.

See also : The future of Northern Ireland : a paper for discussion .(Pages 9-10 in Official Publications Section).

The terror and the tears.
The facts about IRA Brutality and the suffering of victims.
n.d.(c.1972). Belfast. UUP. 16 p.

A pictorial record of the violence.

Continuing the Terror and the Tears.
More facts about the inhumanity of the IRA.
n.d(c.1973). Belfast. UUP. 12 p.

More pictures of the violence, the destruction and the victims.

ULSTER VANGUARD :

> Ulster - A nation .
> 1972. Belfast. Ulster Vanguard. 15 p.
>
> The political organisation, headed by William Craig MP,
> argues here that Ulster could declare UDI if Westminster
> would not agree to the desire of the (Protestant) majo-
> rity in Northern Ireland.
>
> Community of the British Isles.
> 1973. Belfast. Ulster Vanguard . 18 p.
>
> The movement proposes here an independent Ulster within a
> federation of the British Isles.
>
> See also : CRAIG, W : The future of Northern Ireland.
>   (Page 98 in this section).

ULTACH : Orange Terror - The Partition of Ireland.
         1943. Dublin. Capucin Annual. 54 p.
         (reprinted from the Capucin Annual. 1942).

> Ultach is probably the pen-name of Ambrose McCauley.
>
> This is a violent and detailed attack against the Unionist
> Governments of Northern Ireland. There are numerous examples
> of discrimination against Roman Catholics. There is also a
> long list of comments by prominent personalities among whom
> George Noble Count Plunkett and Madame Maud Gonne-McBride.
> In January 1944 this pamphlet was banned in Northern Ireland
> by the Government. The Rev. Professor Corkey, Leader of the
> House in the Ulster Senate, said the publication in its " en-
> tirety was definitely considered to be prejudicial to the pre-
> servation of peace in Northern Ireland ".
>
> Essential reading.
>
> See also : KERR, Rev.W.S : Slanders on Ulster, reply to the
>   " Orange Terror ". (Page 108 in
>   this section).
>
>   ULTACH : The persecutions of catholics in North-
>   ern Ireland. (Page 88 in Articles Sec-
>   tions).

UTLEY, T. E : Ulster - A short background analysis.
              1972. Belfast. Unionist Research Department. (Second edition
              24 p.

> The author is a leader writer of the London based Daily Tele -
> graph, a conservative newspaper. He stood unsuccessfully as
> a Unionist candidate (Pro-Faulkner) for the General Elec-
> tions of February 1974 in North Antrim.
> In this pamphlet he outlines the basic belief of Ulster Unio-
> nists in the maintenance of the link with Great Britain.

WALMSLEY, A. J : <u>Northern Ireland : its policies and record.</u>
n.d (c.1959). Belfast. Ulster Unionist Council. 20 p.

The author, a former member of the Northern Ireland Senate, argues that " Northern Ireland is one of the great successes of modern European Democracies ".

WHYTE, John : <u>Governing without Consensus.</u> A critique.
1972. Belfast. NICRC. 19 p.

Six Northern Ireland academics give their views on Professor Richard Rose's study on Northern Ireland and the author comments on their remarks.

See also : ROSE, R : <u>Governing without consensus.</u>(Page 43 in Selected Works Section).

WILSON, Alec : <u>PR Urban elections in Ulster 1920.</u>
With an introduction and commentary by Robert A. Newland.
1922. New edition : 1972. London. The Electoral Reform Society of Great Britain and Ireland. 63 p.

Proportional Representation by Single Transferable vote was introduced in Ulster in 1920 and abolished in 1922 for local government. The first PR elections for Parliament in Northern Ireland were held in May 1921 and were abolished after the General Elections of 1925.
This work is an account of the urban elections held under PR in 1920 with statements of the actual voting in the various wards in Belfast.
Robert Newland of the Electoral Reform Society asks for the adoption of PR in Northern Ireland.

See also : KNIGHT, J : <u>Northern Ireland - The Elections of the Twenties.</u> (Page 108 in this Section).

LAKEMAN, E : <u>Proportional Representation in Northern Ireland.</u> (Page 78 in Articles Section).

WORKERS ASSOCIATION for the democratic settlement of the national conflict in Ireland.

This association which had its AGM in May 1972 is probably closely associated with the B & ICO.

<u>Why a divided working class</u> ?
1972. Belfast. W.A 29 p.

The Workers Association's policy :" That the mutual recognition of national rights by both nations in Ireland, and the thorough democratic reform of both states, is the only framework within which the national conflict can be resolved ".

<u>War-mongering :"The Irish Press" and the troubles in Northern Ireland.</u>
1973. Belfast. W.A 10 p.

The Workers Association attacks the editorial policy of the Dublin based daily newspaper <u>The Irish Press</u>.

<u>One island, two nations.</u>
1973. Belfast. W.A. 41 p.

This pamphlet was probably written by Rosamund Mitchell. She argues that the Ulster Protestant community has the right to remain within the UK for as long as it wishes.

Essential reading.

<u>Why Articles 2 & 3 must go.</u>
n.d. (c. 1974) . Belfast. W.A. 23 p.

This pamphlet attacks articles 2 & 3 of the Constitution of 1937 of the Republic of Ireland referring to " the national territory " as " the whole of Ireland ".

<u>The Ulster General Strike.</u>
1974 . Belfast. W.A. 10 p.

A collection of the daily bulletins issued by the Workers Association during the political general strike called by the Ulster Workers Council from May 15 to May 29, 1974.
In the Strike Bulletin No 9 (published on May 27) there is an explanation of the W.A and its relation with the UWC.

Essential reading .

See also : RED PATRIOT : <u>The analysis of the significance of</u>
<u>the UWC strike.</u>(Page 117 in this
section).

<u>What's wrong with Ulster Trade Unionism</u> ?
1974. Belfast. W.A. 27 p.

The pamphlet is presented as " an exposure of anti-partitionist manoeuvre and disruption in the trade union leadership ". The anonymous author (probably Boyd Black) sets out to show that the present Official Trade Union leadership in Northern Ireland " is involved in political action which is contrary to the wishes of the vast majority of their members ". This is a direct reference to the ' Back-to-Work ' march organised at the beginning of the strike by Union leaders including Len Murray, General Secretary of the TUC.

See also entry above.

1 - <u>NOVELS</u>

AYLOTT, Bob : <u>Cry for Tomorrow</u> - An Ulster Love Tragedy .
1974. London. Everest Book. 125 p.

British soldier weds a Roman Catholic girl from Belfast. They
leave Ulster to escape from terrorists and go to England where
the IRA shoots them dead.

BALLINGER, W. A : <u>The Green Grassy slopes.</u>
1969. London. Corgi Books. 320 p.

Bible-belt type reverend starts revival campaign in the docks
and shipyards areas of Protestant East Belfast. The author has
obviously modelled his character on the Rev.Ian Paisley.

BARLOW, James : <u>Both your houses.</u>
1971. London. Hamish Hamilton. 274 p.

20 year old Birmingham private in the British Army falls in
love with the daughter of an unemployed Roman Catholic member of the IRA in Belfast. Very vivid descriptions of street
rioting.

BARTON, Harry : <u>Yours till Ireland explodes, Mr Mooney.</u>
1973. Belfast. Blackstaff Press. 114 p.

The hilarious adventures of a 10,000 year old Leprechaun,
Public Relations Officer of the Queens Own Loyal Sinn Fein
Republican Volunteers. A satirical comment on Irish politics during the last 5 years. This is a collection of weekly broadcasts on Northern Ireland radio (BBC) during the
winter.

BARTON, Harry : <u>Yours again Mr Mooney.</u>
1974. Belfast. Blackstaff Press. 96 p.

Mr Mooney's adventures during 1974.

BIRMINGHAM, George A : <u>The Red Hand of Ulster.</u>
1912 . London.
1973. Dublin. Irish University Press (new edition).

G. A. Birmigham is the pseudonym of a Church of Ireland cler-
gyman, the Rev.James Hannay, born in Ulster.
This novel tries to discredit Ulster Unionism by depicting
in detail the horrors which would occur if the Unionists
took to the streets in opposition to Lord Asquith's Home
Rule Bill.

See also : STEWART, A.T.Q : <u>The Ulster Crisis.</u> (Page 44 in
Selected Works Section).

BREWSTER, David : <u>The Heart's Grown Brutal.</u>
1972. London. Angus & Robertson. 218 p.

David Brewster is the pseudonym of a BBC journalist, John Bierman, who has worked several times in Northern Ireland. In the novel, a British journalist is assigned to cover Ulster in July - August 1971. The story culminates with the introduction of internment without trial on August 9, 1971.

See also : MacGUFFIN, J : <u>Internment !</u> (Page 38 in Selected Works Section).

CARRICK, James : <u>With O'Leary in the grave.</u>
    1971. London. Heinemann. 234 p.

Londonderry born policeman in the English Force returns in the Roman Catholic ghetto of the Bogside at the time of the rioting of August 1969 and gets involved in the fighting against the RUC and the British Army and some Protestant extremists.

DE VERE WHITE, Terence : <u>The distance and the dark</u> .
    1973. London. V.Gollancz. 320 p.

The author is Literary Editor of the Dublin based daily <u>the Irish Times</u>.
Rich Protestant farmer in the Republic of Ireland is slowly affected by the present troubles in the North. In spite of his background, he is loyal to the Irish ideal, but he rejects the methods of the Provisional IRA .

DRISCOLL. Peter : <u>In connection with Kilshaw.</u>
    1974. London. MacDonald. 320 p.

Protestant extremists and British Army Intelligence in Belfast today.

FARRELL, J. G : <u>Troubles.</u>
    1970. London. J.Cape. 780 p.

Novel set during the " Troubles ", the civil war in Ireland from 1922 to 1923.

FOLEY, Donal : <u>The best of ' Man Bites Dog '.</u> No 1
    1972. Dublin. Irish Times. 68 p.

<u>The best of ' Man Bites Dog '.</u> No 2
1973. Dublin. Irish Times. 112 p.

<u>The best of ' Man Bites Dog '.</u> No 3
1974. Dublin. Irish Times. 120 p.

Reprints of the weekly, witty and satirical,columns of the News Editor of <u>the Irish Times</u>.

GAILLIE, Menna : <u>You're welcome to Ulster !</u>
    1970. London. V.Gollancz. 238 p.

In 1969 a young Welsh woman visits Roman Catholic friends in
Ulster on the eve of the traditional Orange day - The Twelfth
of July - and gets involved with the IRA and the Protestant
extremists.

HEGARTY, Walter : <u>The price of chips.</u>
1973. London. Davis - Poynter . 249 p.

Two Roman Catholic boys grow up in the ghetto of the Bogside in Londonderry. From 1930 to 1971. The period from 1968
to 1971 follows closely historical events : civil rights
marchs, rioting in August 1969, the split in the IRA, the
role of the British Army,etc...

HERRON, Shaun : <u>Through the dark and hairy wood.</u>
1973. London. J.Cape. 206 p.

British Intelligence and Protestant extremist who wants to
become Prime Minister of Northern Ireland. The action takes
place in 1969.
The author was born in Ulster and now lives in Canada.

HERRON, Shaun : <u>The whore-mother.</u>
1973. London. J.Cape. 281 p.

Young Roman Catholic American graduate joins the Provisional
IRA in Belfast. He soon decides to quit. His escape through
Ireland and England doesn't last long. He is finally shot
dead by the IRA.
For another view of the Provisionals, see : McGUIRE, M :
                              <u>To take Arms.</u> A year in the Provisio-
                              nal IRA. (Page 39 in Selected Works
                              Section).

HIGGINS, Jack : <u>The savage day.</u>
1972. London. Collins. 223 p.

Ex-British Army Major is recruited by HM Forces to recover
half a million in bullion hijacked by the Provisional IRA
in Northern Ireland.

KIELY, Benedict : <u>Modern Irish Fiction</u> - A critique.
1950. Dublin.

This work contains several biographies and bibliographies of
Ulster writers.

LESLIE, Peter : <u>The Extremists.</u>
1970. London. New English Library. 116 p.

British Army Officer, searching for the sniper who killed his
best friend, finds himself caught between Protestant and Roman Catholics extremists in 1969 in Belfast.

LINGARD, Joan : <u>The Lord on our side.</u>
1970. London. Hodder & Stoughton. 223 p.

Life in working-class and middle-class Belfast in the 1960's.

LINGARD, Joan :

> The following titles are part of a trilogy on the present
> troubles for juvenile readers.
> In Belfast a Roman Catholic teenage boy, Kevin, and a Protes-
> tant teenage girl, Sadie, fall in love and escape to London.

> The Twelfth day of July. (1)
> 1970. London. Hamish Hamilton. 127p.

> Across the barricades. (2)
> 1972. London. Hamish Hamilton. 174 p.

> Into Exile. (3)
> 1973. London. Hamish Hamilton. 173 p.

McLAVERTY, Michael : Call my brother back.
> 1939. Dublin. A. Figgis.
> 1970. Dublin. A. Figgis. (Second edition). 261 p.

> Poor Roman Catholic family moves from Rathlin Island (off the
> northern coast of County Antrim) to Belfast. Vivid descript-
> ion of poverty and sectarian strife of the 1920's before the
> setting up of the state of Northern Ireland in 1921.

MARCUS, David (ed.) : Tears of the shamrock.
> 1972. London. Tom Wolfe. 219 p.

> An anthology of contemporary short stories on the them of Ire-
> land's struggle for nationhood. From 1900 to the present day
> in Northern Ireland.

MAXWELL, D. E. S : Imagining the North : violence and the writers.
> pp. 91 - 107
> in Eire-Ireland. St Paul (Minnesota). Vol.8. No 2. 1973.

> The present troubles as seen by writers.

QUINN, Owen : From a Belfast Journal.
> pp. 20 - 36
> in Dublin Magazine. Autumn / Winter 1973-74. Vol.10 No3

> A literary and personal diary.

ST. JORRE, John de, & SHAKESPEARE, Brian : The patriot game.
> 1973. London. Hodder & Stoughton. 256 p.

> James Grogan, son of an Irish freedom-fighter, disillusioned
> with the incompetence of the gun-men of the IRA and disguted
> with the civilian bombings, decides to take events into his
> own hands.He is then the target of the IRA, the RUC, the Bri-
> tish Special Branch.

TARGET, W : <u>The Patriots</u>.
    1974. London. Duckworth. 303 p.

    This novel describes what drives Irish terrorists to plant
    bombs in London. It mixes actuality and fiction to give a
    portrait of a young Irish couple belonging to the IRA. Du-
    ring the summer of 1974 British police were looking for
    such a couple suspected to have planted several bombs in
    England.

WADDELL, Martin : <u>A little bit British</u>. Being the diary of an Ulster-
    man. August 1969.
    1970. London. Tom Stacey. 159 p.

    The diary of Augustus Harland of Boyne Villas, Belfast, kept
    during the month of August 1969 which saw the eruption of vio-
    lence in Northern Ireland. The character is a bigot of the
    extreme kind. Much of the work is documentary and some of
    the material has been taken from factual reports in the
    <u>Belfast Telegraph</u> and the <u>Newsletter</u>.
    Witty satire.

WITHERSPOON, Charles : <u>A sea of troubles</u>.
    1973. Belfast. Blackstaff Press. 123 p.

    A collection of short stories dealing with the present trou-
    bles in Belfast.

BELL, Sam Hannah : <u>The theatre in Ulster.</u>
    1971. Dublin. Gill & MacMillan. 148 p.

    An account - from 1902 to the present day - of what has been
    achieved by both amateur groups and professional companies in
    Ulster.
    Good reference work.

BOYD, John : <u>The Flats.</u>
    1973. Belfast. Blackstaff Press. 86 p.

    This play, performed at the Lyric Theatre of Belfast in 1971,
    deals with a Roman Catholic family living in a block of flats
    situated - obviously - at the top of the Protestant Shankill
    Road in Belfast. They are surroundered by Protestant, Roman
    Catholics gunmen and the British Army.

FRIEL, Brian : <u>The Freedom of the City.</u>
    1974. London. Faber & Faber. 96 p.

    This play is set in Londonderry in 1970. An unauthorised Civil
    Rights March is dispersed with CS Gas and three demonstrators
    take refuge in the Town Hall. Opened first at the Abbey Thea-
    tre in Dublin on February 20,1973. It bears a striking resem-
    blance with the events in Londonderry on January 30,1972,when
    13 civilians were killed by the British Army.

SPEERS, Neil : <u>Drama & theatre in time of conflict & violence.</u>
    pp. 58 - 62
    in <u>Aquarius.</u> Benburb. 1974.

    A look at the way theatre has expressed the concerns and anx-
    ieties of Northern Ireland in the recent years.

THOMPSON, Sam : <u>Over the Bridge.</u>
    Edited and introduced by Stewart Parker.
    1970. Dublin. Gill & Macmillan.

    The play was first produced in 1963 in Belfast.
    The author who worked in the Belfast shipyard,describes the
    sectarian divisions of the work force there who,traditional-
    ly, was predominantly Protestant.

Since 1968 about twenty plays on the troubles have been produced, North and South, but have not yet been published.

BROPHY, Michael : <u>A tired tribe</u>.
        1974. Belfast. Blackstaff Press. 74 p.

        A collection of poems bearing on the dilemma of reconciling
        old loyalties with new aspirations. See especially " Guns
        for the boys ".

DEANE, Seamus : <u>Gradual Wars</u>.
        1972. Dublin. Irish University Press.

FIACC, Padraig : <u>Odour of Blood</u>.
        1973. Goldsmith Press. Dublin.

FIACC, Padraig (ed.) : <u>The wearing of the black</u>.
        1974. Belfast. Blackstaff Press. 174 p.

        An anthology of contemporary Ulster poetry.
        From the editor's introduction : this collection " merely poses
        the question by presenting poets touched by,or involved in,the
        situation here, and suggests how they have tried to come to
        terms with it in their poetry ".
        Poems from 60 poets from Northern Ireland and about 10 from
        Britain, the USA and the Republic of Ireland .
        The anthology is divided in four parts. The first one deals
        with the prehistoric days of the Bog People to 1969. The
        second part centres on Londonderry. The third one covers
        the bombings,the assassinations, the torture in Belfast.
        The fourth one contains poems dealing with the bitterness
        stemming from the results of violence.
        Useful biographies and index to poets.

HEWITT, John : <u>An Ulster reckoning</u>.
        1971. Coventry. Published by the author.

HEWITT, John & MONTAGUE, John : <u>The Planter & the Gael</u>.
        1970. Belfast. Arts Council of Northern Ireland.

KINSELLA, Thomas : <u>Butcher's dozen : A lesson for the octave of Widgery</u>.
        1972. Dublin. Dolmen Press. 8 p.

        Following the publication of the official inquiry by Lord Wid-
        gery (See page 9 In Official Publications Section)on the
        events in Londonderry on January 30,1972 leading to the deaths
        of 13 civilians, Ireland's leading poet published his version
        of the events.

MAHON, Derek : <u>Poetry in Northern Ireland</u>.
        pp. 89 - 93
        in <u>Twentieth Century Studies</u>. Nov.1970. University of Kent.
        Canterbury.

        The new Northern poets.

MONTAGUE, John : <u>The rough field</u>.
      1972. Dublin. Dolmen Press.

MORTON, Robin : <u>Folksongs sung in Ulster</u>.
      1970. Cork. Mercier Press. 95 p.

      50 old and recent folksongs , many previously unpublished .
      Useful appendix of songbooks and records.

ORANGE CROSS : <u>Book of songs, poems and verse</u>.
      n.d (c.1972) Belfast. Orange Cross . 33 p.

      Poems written by Loyalist (ie.Protestant) prisoners jailed
      on charges related to the present troubles.
      The Orange Cross is a charitable organisation which looks
      after the welfare of Loyalist prisoners.

ORANGE SONGS : <u>Orange songs and ballads</u>.
      n.d. London. Toman Music Publishers. 10 p.

      A collection of some of the most famous Orange songs.

PEOPLE'S DEMOCRACY : <u>Songs from the barricades</u>. Vol.1
      n.d (1974). Belfast. PD. 28 p.

      Some of the most famous songs sung by the Roman Catholic
      community since 1968. Most of them are traditional Repu-
      blican songs to which new lyrics have been added.

ST. CLAIR, Sheila : <u>Folklore of the Ulster people</u>.
      1972. Cork. Mercier Press.

SHANKILL DEFENCE ASSOCIATION : <u>Orange Loyalist songs 1971</u> .
      1971. Belfast. SDA. 36 p.

      This Loyalist movement was founded in 1969 by John McKeague
      who was responsible for this publication. It is a collection
      of songs , some of which are fiercely anti-Roman Catholic.
      In May 1971 copies were sent to the British Home Secretary
      and to the Attorney General of Northern Ireland asking for
      proceedings to be taken under the Prevention of Incitement
      to Hatred Act (N.I) 1970. Later John MacKeague was charged
      but released as the jury had disagreed.

SIMMONS, James : <u>West Strand visions</u>.
      1974. Belfast. Blackstaff Press.

      18 poems and 23 lyrics (but not the scores) of his songs.
      See especially " Claudy " : On July 31, 1972 three car-bombs
      exploded without warning killing six people in this little
      village, 12 miles from Londonderry.

ULSTER VOLUNTEER FORCE : <u>A special category</u>. Book of Poems and Verse.
      n.d. (c.1973) Belfast. 35 p.

      This booklet was compiled in Long Kesh by a Red Hand Comman-

do - UVF Prisoner of war, says the second title.
The UVF is a Protestant paramilitary organisation. For more
information see : BOULTON, David : <u>The UVF. 1966 - 1973</u>.(Page
21 in Selected works section).

WATTERS, Loughlin : <u>Omen of Lagan. Belfast 1971.</u>
    1972. Dublin.

    The river Lagan runs through Belfast.

WHITE, Marion and McCORRY, Jim and SMYTH, Sam (editors):
    <u>Love Orange, Love Green.</u>
    Poems of living, loving and dying working-class Ulster.
    1974. Belfast. Whitcor Publications. 100 p.

    Loyalist and Republican poems.

SECTION C : INDEX OF AUTHORS